THE NOTE

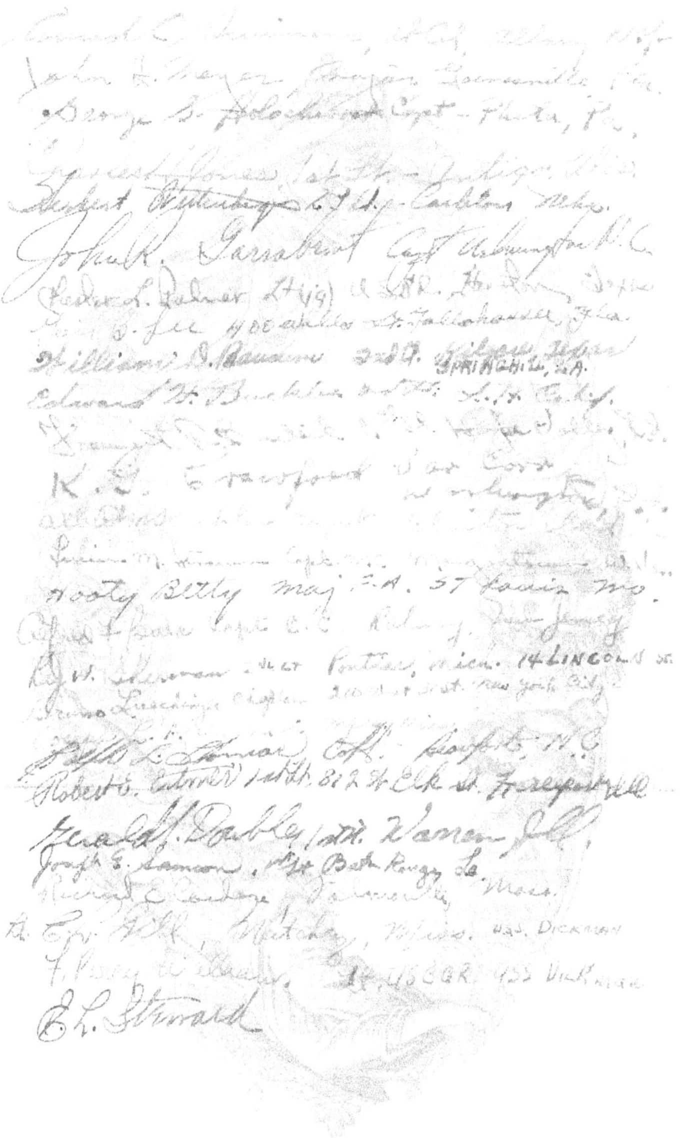

by Stephen Cano

i

Design and production services for this book were provided
by Linden Publishing, Fresno, CA. 800-345-4447.

Contents

For Michele

Capt. Robert C. Crisson

The Note

Captain Robert C. Crisson could not believe his eyes. He had just opened his military trunk for the first time since the D-Day invasion of Normandy on June 6, 1944. On that fateful day, Captain Crisson was hit with shrapnel from a German 88 (an 88-millimeter cannon) and wounded in the left leg. The shrapnel also hit a red smoke grenade in his gear, which when combined with the water, made it look like he was bleeding all over. The medics thought he was dead, so they took all his personal effects and sent them to Kansas City, where the military stored the belongings of its deceased. All of Captain Crisson's highly classified maps and codes were sent there and a couple months later to his mother's house, where they stayed until a couple of years after the war. One day, Captain Crisson's mother turned to him and said, "Would you look in this old foot locker?" And there they were. His secret maps and codes which he framed and proudly hung in his house. [1] Inside this trunk were many war artifacts and, of course, memories, including a large French Cino Cents Francs banknote, signed by a number of unknown men. Years later and after Captain Crisson had passed away, I became friends with his daughter, Michele, who graciously gifted me this French banknote in appreciation of my remembrance of her father and our friendship. After much research and to my astonishment, I began uncovering story after story. These men were not simply war-time friends but rather all intertwined through the historic D-Day invasion of June 6, 1944. I began to see Captain Crisson's banknote in an entirely different light. This was a work of art – from the fascinating stories behind each

---

[1] The News Tribune, Issue No. 56, 1994, Al Gibbs

1

signature, to the selection of the French banknote type. Captain Crisson's French banknote began a D-Day story that would take on a life of its own, bringing to light new stories of the greatest generation in American history.

—Stephen P. Cano

1st Battalion - 8th Infantry Regiment - 4th Infantry Division - D- Day Utah Beach - June 6, 1944

Lt. Col. Conrad Christopher Simmons
Albany, New York
1st Battalion Commander
Silver Star / Purple Heart
Killed in Action - June 24, 1944

Major John Henry Meyer
Gainesville, Florida
Executive Officer - 1st Battalion
Silver Star
Died 12-03-2001

Captain George Gregory Holochwost Philadelphia, Penn
29th Field Artillery (8th Infantry Regiment)
Wounded in Action – June 6, 1944
Silver Star
Died 6-13-1976

1st Lt. Charles Harmon Jones DSC
Antigo, Wisconsin
1st Battalion Headquarter (Staff Intelligence Officer)
Distinguished Service Cross / Purple Heart
Killed in Action - June 10, 1944

2nd Lt. Herbert Walker Wittenberger
Carleton, Nebraska
1st Battalion Staff
Wounded in Action – June 1944
Became S-2 10/44
Died 6-20-1947

Captain John Richard Garrabrant
Wilmington, North Carolina
1st Battalion Headquarter Staff
Distinguished Service Cross / Purple Heart
Kill in Action – June 10, 1944

Lt. Chester Leroy Palmer
Houston, TX
USNR (United States Naval Reserve)
Seriously Wounded in Action – June 8, 1944
Died 12-16-1997

1st Lt. Gail Bruce Lee
Tallahassee, Florida
Commander B Company
Distinguished Service Cross /Bronze Star/Purple Heart
Wounded in Action – June 12, 1944
 Died 2-21-1970

2nd Lt. William Dayton Baucum
Springhill, Louisiana
C Company – Boat 7
Seriously Wounded in Action June 10,1944
Died 9-07-1985

2nd Lt. Edward Henry Buckles
Long Beach, California
Purple Heart
Killed in Action – September 20, 1944

2nd Lt. Fremont Ralph Burdick
Oak Valley, Rhode Island
 C Company – Boat 9
Seriously Wounded in Action – June 9, 1944
Bronze Star
Died 8-09-1977

Kenneth Gale Crawford
War Correspondent
First newsman to wade ashore on Normandy on D-Day
Died 1-14-1983

Capt. Albert Matthews Krekler
Clinton, Indiana
6th Armored Group
70th Tank Battalion
Wounded in Action five times (6-44, 7-15-44, 8-7-44, 9-29-44)
Silver Star, Purple Heart (5 Clusters), Bronze Star
Died 1-31-1981

Capt. Lucien Martin Strawn
Medical Corps.
Morgantown, West Virginia
Battalion Surgeon
Silver Star
Died 11-12-1988

Major Hutson "Hooty" Miller Betty
St. Louis, Missouri
Special Staff – Special Service Officer - Field Artillery
Died 4-08-1991

Capt. Alfred Francis Birra
Rahway, New Jersey
 C.E.(Combat Engineer)
Company C 237th Engineer Combat Battalion
Died 6-20-1984

2nd Lt. Ray William Sherman
Pontiac, Michigan
Wounded in Action – June 15, 1944
Purple Heart
Killed in Action – June 24, 1944

Captain Bruno Luechinger
New York City, New York
1st Battalion Chaplain
Silver Star – June 9, 1944
Died 7-20-1961

2nd Lt. Joseph Phillip Kirby
Minneapolis, Minnesota
C Company - Boat 10
Lightly Wounded in Action – June 8, 1944
Died 10-31-1963

Captain Ralph Lester Thomas
Beauford, North Carolina
1st Battalion Staff
Silver Star/Bronze Star/Purple Heart
Died 12-20-2008

1st Lt Robert Elwood Ertmer
Freeport, Illinois
1st Battalion
Evacuated due to Exhaustion – June 1944
Died 10-19-1980

1st Lt. Gerald Showers Doubler
Warren, Illinois
Evacuated due to Exhaustion - June 15, 1944
Died 2-08-1989

1st Lt. Joseph Edwards Samson
Baton Rouge, Louisiana
Commander D Company
Wounded in Action – June 22, 1944
Died 12-28-1972

2nd Lt. Richard Eugene Cardoze
Falmouth, Massachusetts
Silver Star – June 10, 1944
Died 11-04-1992

Lt. Edgar Lawrence Gill
Natchez, Mississippi
U.S.S. Dickman
Died 12-10-1981
USCG

Lt. Fendall Perry Williams
Richmond, Virginia
U.S.S. Dickman
USCCR
Died 4-04-1991

B.L. ,Steward

French note originally owned by Capt. Robert Crisson, Commander C
Company on D Day.

Capt. Robert Carl
Crisson
Birmingham, Alabama
Commander C Company
Slightly Wounded in Action – June 6 , 1944, July 1944, October 1944
Silver Star (June 6, 1944)
Distinguished Service Cross – July 30, 1944
Purple heart (three Clusters)
Died 11-16-2013

Men Are Called

The granite marker in the Friary cemetery at Sacred heart, Yonkers, will give the "short and simple annals"....Died, July 20, 1961, Age 51, Years in Religious Life 34, Years in the Priesthood 28. But simply reading that marker would never allow one to understand the shock that hit the Province when the telephone calls from St. John's announced his sudden death. Missionaries in the Pacific and in Nicaragua felt his loss. Messages began to pour in, not only from Capuchins, but from members of other religious orders as well. The entire mission world seemed plunged in mourning.[2]

Father Bruno Luechinger was born in New York City, September 25, 1909. His parents, Albert Luechinger and Elizabeth Rauch were natives of Switzerland and Austria respectively. He was one of four children. The family moved from the Bronx to Lindenhurst, Long Island, shortly after Bruno's birth. Bruno's father was a weaver by trade and did monogram orders for department stores, working at home on a hand loom. As a child, Bruno learned the skill and retained his touch with a needle throughout his life. When he was nine years old his mother died. His father passed away a few years later leaving him an orphan. But by this time Bruno was in the Sacred Heart Serephicate, Yonkers, preparing for the priesthood.[3]

Bruno Luechinger's contact with the Order came through his father. The Capuchin's are a revered name in Switzerland. Bruno's father himself was a Third order member. When Bruno expressed his desire to become a priest his good father led him to the Capuchin's. He began his preparatory studies

---

[2] Tribute to Father Bruno, Father Julius Sullivan, O.F.M. Cap.

[3] Tribute to Father Bruno, Father Julius Sullivan, O.F.M. Cap.

in September 1921. He was barely twelve years old at the time. He was a sturdy lad of light complexion, dark hair, rosy cheeks and large wide-awake brown eyes. He was a bright student who applied himself well. He was also deft at the cleaning and maintenance tasks that are traditionally expected of aspirants. He was not athletically minded, though he did mix in handball contests and basketball shooting for holy pictures and enjoyed taking long hikes. He spent six years of his seminary training at St. Anthony Friary, Marathon, Wisconsin. There he made excellent progress in his studies and manifested special aptitude for library management under the skilled guidance of father Sylvester Brielmeier who would go on to become librarian of the Capuchin International College in Rome. The class was ordained to the priesthood June 25, 1933.[4]

Father Bruno's first assignment was to Glenclyffe as prefect of discipline in the High School. He also taught physics, mathematics and history. In 1938 he was relieved of the prefect job but continued as instructor. He also served as secretary to Father Benedict, the Rector. The negotiation and paper work involved in having the High School accredited with the New York State Board of Regents were his achievement. At the same time, he was not above such muscular tasks as sanding and varnishing floors during the holidays. One of Father Bruno's diversions was the compositions of Latin lyrics to the metre of "Iste Confessor" and he joined merrily in signing them for feast days of the professors.[5]

While stationed at Garrison, Father Bruno kept up a week-end help out at St. Sebastian's parish in Woodside, Long Island. It was on one of these trips that he became acquainted with the O'Mara family, a clan of nine with three brothers' priests. The O'Maras "adopted" Father Bruno as a fourth priest-son. Father Bruno responded to their friendship and regarded the O'Mara home as his own. He wrote to them constantly while in the service and the family offered a daily prayer for his safety before a statue of the Blessed Virgin in the foyer of their home where a vigil lamp burned constantly.[6]

Before entering the service as army chaplain, Father Bruno spent a year (1942-43) as Director of the Third Order of St. John's. His happy-going manner and clear, solid sermons endeared him to the large fraternity with

---

[4] Tribute to Father Bruno, Father Julius Sullivan, O.F.M. Cap.

[5] Tribute to Father Bruno, Father Julius Sullivan, O.F.M. Cap.

[6] Tribute to Father Bruno, Father Julius Sullivan, O.F.M. Cap.

which he worked. But his stay was short and in July 1943, he received his commission and was attached to the Eight Infantry Regiment, Fourth Division. When he joined his regiment, which was training in the South, he was pleased to find that quite a number of the men were from his midtown Manhattan.[7]

By the early part of 1944 the regiment was in England awaiting the planned invasion of Europe. David Howarth, in his book, "D-Day, the Sixth of June 1944" makes favorable mention of Father Bruno. We gather that his men were loyally attached to him and the English at Devon delighted in his good-natured ribbing. Writes David Howarth: "Even if he had not been a friar, Luechinger would have been a remarkable person; for he was not only a very learned man, but was also a master of the opulent slang which is the hallmark of the true New Yorker. His own troops found it easy to confide in a priest who naturally spoke their own language, and spoke it more fluently than they did." His friendliness went further than words. From another source we know that Father Bruno had permission from his Provincial to use his salary to procure hard-to-get comforts for the men and for cases of need that came to his attention. Miss Mae O'Mara was his faithful agent in New York. Once Father Bruno had to ask her not to put soap and tea in the same package.[8]

As a young man growing up in Richmond, Charlottesville and Clifton Forge, Virginia, Fendall Perry Williams attitude towards school and teachers was very bad at times. But his Clifton Forge High School principal saw something promising in Williams if only the right guidance could be provided. So, he recommended Williams to the Virginia Military Institute. He felt discipline in a military school was exactly what he needed.[9] He was right. Williams enrolled in the VMI in 1928 and received a B.A. degree in Liberal Arts in 1932. He served as a 2nd Lieutenant in the U.S. Army Field Artillery Reserve for two years active duty and another four years as a 2nd Lieutenant in the U.S. Marine Corps Reserve. When the United States entered World War II, he was commissioned a lieutenant in the U.S. Coast Guard Reserve serving on the USS Joseph T Dickman from May 1942 until September 1946 at which time he was released as a Lt.

---

[7] Tribute to Father Bruno, Father Julius Sullivan, O.F.M. Cap.

[8] Tribute to Father Bruno, Father Julius Sullivan, O.F.M. Cap.

[9] Certificate of Recommendation for Admission to Virginia Military Institute, Principal E.W. Miller, Clifton Forge High School

Commander. Williams participated as a Beach Master Commander in five amphibious D-Day Landings including Gela, Sicily in July 1943, at Salerno in September 1943, at Utah Beach on D-Day, June 6, 1944, in Southern France in August 1944 and in the Pacific at Okinawa on Easter Sunday, 1945. He received a commendation from Commander of Transports for service in the Sicily Landings where he was the Beach Master Commander of Dickman's shore party for the First Ranger Battalion landing at Gela, Sicily. He received Combat Stars for five "D" Day Landings. On the USS Dickman, Williams service included Watch Officer, Division Officer and Beach Master Commander.[10]

But on May 26, 1944, the USS Dickman was still to take part in the largest amphibious operation of all, "Operation Neptune", or the invasion of Normandy. The U.S.S. Joseph T. Dickman reported to Falmouth, England, on May 26, 1944, together with the U.S.S. Barnet and H.M.S. Empire Gauntlet. From this base these vessels, as part of Task Force Utah, proceeded to Plymouth Harbor and then to Tor Bay anchorage on May 31, 1944.[11] Here the loading of vehicles and cargo was carried out. On June 1, 1944, Lt. Richard E. Cardoze (8th Infantry Regiment) reported aboard as T.Q.M. (Total Quality Management), for pending operations.[12] About a week earlier, Major John H. Meyer, the 8th Infantry Regiment Executive Officer and U.S. Military Academy West Point 1939 graduate, and Lt. Joseph E. Samson, Commander D Company, 8th Infantry Regiment, came aboard the Dickman as Army transport quartermasters, and completed duties aboard the Dickman in preparation for the invasion.[13]

Also reporting aboard on June 1st was Kenneth Crawford, U.S. War Correspondent. Crawford, a Sparta, Wisconsin native, would be the first newsman to wade ashore in Normandy on D-Day in 1944. He went to work for United Press in Chicago in 1924 after graduating from Beloit College in Wisconsin. He came to Washington for the United Press in 1927 and was immediately assigned to cover the White House.[14] Eventually, he would become a confidant of presidents from Roosevelt to Nixon. He became a Newsweek columnist and thus reported for them during the

---

[10] Virginia Military Institute Register Confirmation 1989 Register of Former Cadets

[11] U.S.S. Joseph T. Dickman Log

[12] U.S.S. Joseph T. Dickman Log

[13] U.S.S. Joseph T. Dickman Log

[14] Kingsport Times News (Kingsport, Tennessee) 1/14/83

D-Day invasion. "I first heard the details of the plan of campaign, on the afternoon of June 1, 1944. A group of war correspondents accredited to the Navy were transported to the headquarters of Rear Admiral Alan G. Kirk, Commander of the United States invasion task force. He told us the whole thing would be risky, no matter how carefully planned. Much depended upon the weather, but if D Day had to be postponed many more days, the tides would not be right again for about a month. A month's delay might eliminate all the elements of surprise. He was confident, he said, that once initial landings were made, all would go well. The night I went aboard the USS Dickman I reported to the executive officer. My orders permitted me to go ashore following the initial waves, with the Navy beachmaster. "Why not go on first and see the whole show?" I was asked by an Army officer who said that he himself had been ordered to go later but would prefer to go first if he had a choice. "I have the chart right here. I'll put you down for boat 14." "Good," I said. "Mighty kind of you. First it is."[15] Both Cardoze and Crawford would come ashore on D-Day. Both men would have met Lt. F. Perry Williams and Lt. E.G. Gill who had joined the Coast Guard in 1940.

On June 4th, 1944, Capt. Robert C. Crisson and the 8th Infantry Regiment First Battalion loaded aboard the U.S.S. Joseph T. Dickman. Crisson was a 23-year-old commander of C Company and would lead this company along with other elements of the 1st Battalion, 8th Infantry Regiment in the 1st wave on Utah Beach on June 6[th, 1944.] Crisson had joined the Alabama National Guard at age 17 and was later assigned to the Army's 4th Infantry Division, where he worked his way up the ranks to become a commissioned officer. By the end of the war, Crisson would be promoted to Major and be the youngest battalion commander in the army.[16] The invasion was originally planned for June 5th but was delayed one day due to weather. So, the invasion was still a few days away. Crisson was quite aware of the historical nature of this moment. He carried on his belongings a large French Cino Cents Francs banknote and once aboard the U.S.S. Dickman, Crisson would have 27 D-Day veterans sign the banknote. Capt. Crisson never signed the French banknote. But like a Mosaic art piece filled with many colorful pieces, Crisson's selection of each man on the note represented something to him. Something much larger than just an individual

---

[15] Newsweek, June 19, 1944: p. 73, Kenneth G. Crawford

[16] New Tacoma, Washington Obituary, November 2013

signature. These men represented virtually every American land and sea element on D-Day that would begin the ground war in Europe. The phrase, "E pluribus unum", Latin for "Out of many, one", was never truer. Crisson knew many of these men would never see American shores again. Their signature on the French banknote was a moment that sealed their historical bond before all men went their separate ways and to their fate.

The banknote included a total of 22 members of the 1st Battalion, 8th Infantry Regiment including the Battalion commander (Lt. Col. Conrad Simmons), Battalion Executive Officer (Major John H Meyer), 3 Company commanders (1st Lt. Gail B. Lee – B Company, 1st Lt. Joseph E. Samson – D Company, and Capt. Robert C. Crisson – C Company), the first Allied Chaplain to land in France (Capt. Bruno Luechinger), four Distinguished Service Cross recipients (1st Lt. Charles H. Jones, Capt. John R. Garrabrant and Capt. Robert C. Crisson, and 1st Lt. Gail B. Lee), and nine Silver Star recipients (Lt. Col. Conrad Simmons, Major John H. Meyer, Capt. George G. Holochwost, Capt. Ralph L. Thomas, Capt. Albert M. Krekler, Capt. Lucien M. Strawn, 2nd Lt. Richard E. Cardoze, Chaplain Bruno Leuchinger and Capt. Robert C. Crisson). Although Crisson did not actually sign the note, it was his note and his idea to have the men sign it. Two men were officers of the U.S.S. Joseph T. Dickman, Lt. E.L. Gill and Lt. F. Perry Williams (Coast Guard Commendation). Another was with the U.S. Navy Naval Demolition Group and served as a spotter for the U.S.S. Nevada on D Day (Lt. Chester L. Palmer). One man was the Steward on the U.S.S. Joseph T. Dickman (initials B.L.). A man from the 70th Tank Battalion signed (Capt. Albert M. Krekler), also signing were 29th Field Artillery (Capt. George G. Holochwost), 1st Battalion Surgeon (Capt. Lucien M. Strawn), and 237th Engineer Combat Battalion (Capt. Alfred F. Birra). And another was the first war correspondent to come ashore on D-Day, Kenneth G. Crawford. At least 21 Purple Hearts were also earned in the group of soldiers. As Capt. Crisson carefully put away the signed French banknote in his personal trunk, one can imagine his thoughts as he turned to the day ahead. On June 5th, 1944, U.S.S. Joseph T. Dickman departed Tor bay for the greatest invasion in the history of the world.

The Fight for Utah Beach

There was little sleep for men of the 8th Infantry Regiment on the night of June 5th and during the early morning of June 6th. It was like the night before the big game. Each man lay in his bunk in the troop compartment or sat on the floor of the recreation room amidship, chain smoking, talking to the man next to him, and anticipating what might befall him within the next twenty-four hours. The crew of the transport prepared hot breakfast for the assault parties which would leave the ships before dawn. A number of men not in the initial assault landings volunteered to assist in serving and preparing the meal. One of these men was particularly receptive to the mood of his comrades on D-Day, and described it thus:[17]

"I was on the USS Dickman with assault elements of the 1st Battalion and attached troops. I was more interested in the psychological reaction of the men with whom I had been intimately associated for two and one-half years, than in volunteering for a dirty job just to be a good guy. I dreaded the coming of H-hour as much as the man who'd hit the beach. I think that I was principally afraid that I might see some of my friends shot up on the beach and on the route of advance inland. As the men came through the chow line between two and three o'clock in the morning of the 6th, they were like high strung race horses, nervous, frightened, some morose. I knew as I spoke to each man that it might be for the last time. They were probably aware of it too, but were a hard-determined looking group, resolved to do their job and oddly enough much less frightened, in much better emotional shape and much better steeled against the things they would see and go

---

[17] 8th Regiment Daily Summaries, June , 1944

through, than many troops attached to us who had been through previous invasions. As the men sat down to eat, all apprehension seemed to vanish abruptly and was replaced by an almost festive mood of troops on maneuvers. After breakfast the men retuned to their quarters, strapped on their equipment and waited on directions of the Dickman's loud speaker system to go to their assault boats. As each man finished breakfast and secured his equipment, he did not have long to wait before being called. There was not much time or opportunity for morbid reflection. Last minute of instruction from his officer, a cigarette and a slap on the back with a word of God speed from his chaplain sent each 8th Infantryman into his boat with a feeling of self-confidence and assurance that the operation would be a great success."[18]

Among the men waiting to go ashore at Utah Beach that morning was Chaplain Bruno Luechinger. Just his presence there as a non-combatant at that crucial moment was in military terms "over and beyond the call of duty." But Chaplain Luechinger had been able to convince the command that the men facing German batteries needed him. And it was with a thankful heart that he would find the casualties that day to be comparatively light.[19]

Capt. Alfred F. Birra had enlisted in the U.S. Army shortly after the Pearl Harbor attack. Born in Brooklyn, New York, he then moved to Rahway, New Jersey to be near his future wife. He was assigned to the 237th Engineer Combat Battalion and now found himself aboard the U.S.S. Joseph T. Dickman on the eve of the Normandy invasion, "We had been aboard ship for three days, living a life of ease and luxury and formulating our final plans when the General came aboard. He made an address to the troops via the PA and left sealed orders with the commander of troops. These orders contained the information as to D-Day and H-Hour. At about five o'clock on the evening of June 5th, it was announced to us that at 0630 on the following morning we would land on the coast of France. The first platoon and the commanding officer of Co. C 237th Engineers would land with the first assault wave. The remainder would come ashore in succeeding waves. We were breeching a concrete seawall and clearing passage ways of obstacles and mines so that the tanks that were landing with us could get off the beach. A very vital point since without the support of the tanks with their

---

[18] 8th Regiment Daily Summaries, June 6, 1944, Pg. 4
[19] Tribute to Father Bruno, Father Julius Sullivan, O.F.M. Cap.

armor and heavy guns, the Infantry would be too busy protecting its own skin to do any real good. Although we knew most of this, it still came as somewhat of a shock, and we set about making last minute preparations."[20]

Capt. Alfred F. Birra continued, "There weren't many who got much sleep that night of June 5th. For the most part, we sat around, talked, played cards, drank coffee and did the usual things a man does when he is worried and a little scared and doesn't want to show it. At 0230 in the morning, breakfast was served, of which most of us partook heartily, since we knew it would be, if not our last meal, at least the last for quite a few hours or perhaps days. At 0330 we began the business of debarking. The weatherman had been, as is wont with that particular breed, very wrong in his prediction. Instead of the smooth, glassy sea he predicted, it was very rough and cold, and the night was inky black so that a man had to feel his way about the ship, stumbling and cursing softly. The small landing craft were loosened from the davits, and each absorbed its crew of men and equipment and was lowered into a black sea, which seemed to reach up with hungry arms to drag the frail craft down. How can I describe the feeling which grips you at this moment? Kent (a fellow soldier) echoed my feeling exactly when he said that this precise moment, when the assault boat was being lowered from the mother ship, was the loneliest time in his life. Not one says a word except the man at the cables. As the boat goes down the rail, the ship disappears, and with a slap that jars everyone aboard, the craft hits the water. The cables are cast off and now you're entirely on your own and alone."[21]

Lt. Col John R. Meyer grew up in his family home, "Promised Land" in Plaquemines Parish, Louisiana. As a West Point graduate, he would lead the 1st Battalion across France through Luxemburg and Germany in five campaigns, "The boats came in from 14,000 yards, 8 or 9 miles. It took 50 minutes. We approached the rendezvous area very slowly behind mine sweepers. And anchored about 0230. In the distance we could hear AA fire and see the searchlights. One C-47 came back right over our ship. The air bombardment came after we anchored. First wave began loading on LSVP's about 0315 – all assault elements (early waves) loaded by 0430. Some rail loaded, 8 boats at a time, also over 4 were net loaded where they entered the boat by climbing down a cargo net. After davits lowered it took 15 minutes to set the next. 8 boats, 3 times (24 boats) rail loaded and the

---

[20] Letter Home From Alfred F. Birra, July 12, 1944

[21] Letter Home From Alfred F. Birra, July 12, 1944

rest were net loaded. This was the roughest sea in any loading and therefore made it very difficult. There were no losses during loading, but plenty of sea-sickness."[22]

Capt. Alfred F. Birra continued, "We chugged away and, in a few seconds, the large mother ship became just a darker blob of darkness and then disappeared from view entirely. It was now time to start for the rendezvous area, where we would meet the rest of the craft that made up our wave. In just a few minutes the spray from the waves slapping the bow and sides of the boat had us all thoroughly drenched, and the men began to snap out of their lethargy only to find themselves miserably seasick. I can safely say that of the thirty men aboard, at least twenty were seasick. I myself didn't have time, nor could I display any form of weakness by getting sick. We were soon at the rendezvous area, and the boats comprising the wave got into their proper positions and began to circle. We were about six miles offshore at this point. Soon things began to happen that made even the most wretched sit up with interest. The show had started. And it started with the Navy. In the distance on all sides we could see the huge sleek forms of battleships and destroyers vomiting flames of fire as their fourteen- and sixteen-inch guns opened fire. The air was filled with deafening roars and the screams of shells. Then the coastal defense batteries opened up and added to the general hubbub. We had no sooner become accustomed to this when over the noise of the battleships we heard the roar of hundreds of motors, the air corps was coming in. And come in they did, literally in waves, and made for the shore and their targets. That their bombs were effective was evidenced by the fires that soon lit up the entire black night. That the enemy was striking back was also soon evidenced by that ack ack that started to crosshatch the sky. The entire picture defies description by my limited senses and no matter how retentive, I could not possibly have absorbed the entire picture and all of the occurrences."[23]

As the dawn wiped away the darkness, the beach became visible against the higher ground and wooded areas of the coast. The Air Force had commenced bombing the beach at H minus five hours and as the dawn became progressively lighter, it was possible to distinguish orange flashes of the bomb bursts in relation to definite positions on the beach. At H minus forty minutes, the battleships Nevada and Enterprise, with supporting

---

[22] 8th Regiment Interviews, Lt. Col. John H. Meyer, CO 1st Battalion, 8th Inf, June 6, 1944

[23] Letter Home From Alfred F. Birra, July 12, 1944

heavy and light cruiser's and destroyers, laid down a devastating barrage of fire on beach strong points and enemy positions commanding the beach and its exits to inland routes of advance. Until 0600 the assault boats which had been loaded with their personnel and equipment several hours previously, had circled their transports awaiting the moment for rendezvous on the basis of their respective assault waves. Approximately one-half hour before H-hour, the first assault waves of the 1st and 2nd Battalion rendezvoused and started toward the beach to predetermined points of landing which were then in the process of being cleared of under water obstacles by specially trained Navy Personnel. It was a marvelous picture; one that almost defies description. It is difficult to imagine the thousands of craft of the invasion fleet, some anchored, and others moving about in the channel off the Cotentin Peninsula. It was the climax of over two years preparation. It was the greatest amphibious operation which had ever been attempted. It was smooth, perfectly coordinated and magnificent, but, the most magnificent thing about it was the men in the assault crafts approaching the beach, their eyes focused on that narrow strip of sand, their rifles loaded and ready for immediate use, their tense expectant bodies anxiously awaiting the moment when the boats would come in through the surf, permitting them to wade ashore, reduce the enemy strong points there and close with the soldiers of the Third Reich in hand to hand combat.[24]

Kenneth Crawford continued, "Guess the folks back home are pretty excited about this," said a voice from the back of the barge as we turned for the final run into the beach where German machine guns, German artillery, and German mines were presumed to be waiting. "Hear they're doing a lot of praying," said another in a depreciating way. Nobody answered. Silence seemed to assent to the foolishness of prayer. I had noticed, however, that chaplains worked overtime holding well-attended services, confessionals, and private conferences just before take-off from our mother ship. The good thing about seasickness," somebody suggested, "is that you don't care if you live or die." Packs were being fastened. There was a stream of curses as straps soaked with sea water refused to come buckled. Six inches of bilge, compounded of sea water and vomit, sloshed forward and aft. Ahead clearly visible in the dank morning light was the 500-yard-wide beach we had studied so often in reconnaissance photographs. To reach their first cover these boys would have to traverse about 25 yards of water, starting

---

[24] 8th Regiment Daily Summaries, June 6, 1944

at waist depth, and then the width of the beach, now shrouded by artillery fire and aerial bombardment. Their first objective would be the retaining wall along the dunes flanking the beach. They expected to fight for the wall when they reached it, and bayonets were fixed for the ordeal. One of my boatmates offered a bag of hand grenades. "Can't use them," I shouted. "War correspondent. Rule against it." "To hell with the rules," he said. "You got to have something if you haven't got a gun." "Wouldn't know how to pull the pin," I answered. He gave me a look that seemed to combine pity with disgust."[25]

Crawford edged close to Capt. Robert Crisson, commander of C Company of the 8th Infantry Regiment, as the LCVP motored closer to the Normandy shoreline and Utah Beach. Crisson had turned twenty-three less than two weeks earlier and was about to enter combat for the first time after five years in the Army.[26] Crawford continued, "Remember what you've been learning for the last three years," said Capt. Robert Crisson in an easy Birmingham voice. "Don't run in water or you'll just wear yourself out. When you hit the beach, run for that wall and let 'em have it. Get some toeholds along that side planking."[27]

Lt. Col. Meyer's boat was leaking, so it turned back and everyone was transferred to a LSVP. The boat pulled alongside a ship and got the compass bearing for the run, then moved in alone. About 500 yards off-shore he found that he was heading for an empty beach; He then saw the fighting a mile away to the left, therefore, he turned south to head for the actual landing beach. He waded ashore through destroyed under-water obstacles.[28]

Kenneth Crawford continued, "Down the ramp! Shouted the coxswain from the elevated stern. Down it came with a clank and splash. Ahead, and it seemed at that moment miles off, stretched the sea wall. At Capt. Crisson's insistence we had all daubed our faces with Commando black. They expected a fight for the wall when they reached it, and bayonets were fixed for the ordeal. I charged out with the rest, trying to look fierce and desperate, only to step into a shell hole and submerge myself in the channel.

---

[25] Newsweek, June 19, 1944, p. 73, Kenneth G. Crawford

[26] ww2ondeadline.com/2020/03/29/d-day-utah-beach-Kenneth-crawford/

[27] Newsweek, June 19, 1944: p. 73, Kenneth G. Crawford

[28] 8th Regiment Interviews, Lt. Col. John H. Meyer, CO 1st battalion, 8th Inf, June 6, 1944

Luckily my gear was too wet and stinking to put on so I was light enough to come up."[29]

Capt. Crisson, "There wasn't a man ahead of me when we crossed that sand. We began working our way down sand dunes looking for said fort. There was a fence around the house. The next thing I knew I was staring right into a big black and white sign that said: 'Achtung! Minen!'" Well I reckon I hesitated just a second then looking at that mine sign, but I glanced to the sides and my boys were piling right over that fence. I thought I was supposed to be encouraging them, but that time, boy, they were encouraging me. I followed them over the fence and we took the house.[30] After a while the radio was burning, NCO reported, "Dammit Captain, there's no fort down here." Small boats to rear of our craft had been firing plenty of machine guns, possibly to destroy mines in our and their path. Having landed we moved on inland to knock out houses along the road back of the dunes. Company "B" took Fort Madeline assisted by Company "C". The left sections of Company C took Fort T7. Little opposition at these forts which apparently did not fire on us. Some small arms fire from houses along the road but the Germans there gave up gladly when we closed in. At this moment a private came running up and said, "I have got two women over here." "Where have you got them?" "In a ditch." "What the hell are you doing with two women in a ditch?" "I don't want them to get shot." A Communications sergeant standing there wanted to know "how old they were." I immediately moved the two women and a male civilian into a safer spot. Established Company C at church (444789). German artillery fire was coming from across the swamps from the direction of le Rivere so I asked for naval supporting fire and tank fire. Tanks wouldn't fire on account of endangering 2nd Battalion. I proceeded inland accompanied by two observers and a runner. Machine guns began firing as we made for a ditch. An artillery shell burst in the middle of the road, killing the two observers and wounding me. The runner was not hurt. After recovering from shock at about 0630 I marched the Company North thru La Madeleine but was unable to continue and was evacuated. Most of the casualties were from mines and 88's, small arms fire from the buildings and on the road back of the dunes.[31] We got off real light on the landing. It was potentially the most

---

[29] Newsweek, June 19, 1944: p. 73, Kenneth G. Crawford

[30] York Herald Tribune, Paris, June 6, 1947

[31] 8th Regiment Interview, Capt. Robert C. Crisson, Commanding Co. C, 8th Inf

dangerous beach. But we had an advantage. We had never been subjected to combat and didn't know enough to be afraid."[32]

Kenneth Crawford continued, "The soldiers were well out of the water, carrying packs, guns, heavy mortar parts, and radio equipment, by the time I made the beach. They crouched low and ran apelike. We had been told to expect booby traps and antipersonnel mines on the beach, machine-gun fire from the dunes, and probably artillery fire from behind them. Strangely, there were no mines and no machine guns. Only artillery fire, and that directed against the boats. We missed our allotted place on the beach by about 800 yards because some of the boats were so water-logged that they couldn't complete the up-beach run. I leaned against the sea wall and looked back over the beach. The second wave was just coming in. As far as I could see to the left and right, they came more slowly this time because they had seen the easy time we had. Too slowly. A shell from the battery of German 88's in a strong point beyond the upper end of the beach had got range. Just in front of me a shell burst in a cluster of seven men. Six crumpled, apparently dead. The seventh screamed in agonized amazement. There were no corpsmen on the beach. When the 88's shifted their fire to another sector, I ran down to help the seventh man. He turned out to be a 200-pounder and beyond my strength to carry. At his suggestion we tried walking, with me as a prop. He had been hit in the arm and leg with shrapnel. Both were broken. "What good am I going to be without an arm and leg?" he asked. "Take it easy," I said. "You'll have your arm and your leg. We must have fallen in a tangle six times before we regained the sea wall and safety. Later, I saw him aboard the evacuation barge. He will have his arm and his leg, but they may not be much good."[33]

Capt. Alfred F. Birra, "Dawn has broken, and dimly in a haze of smoke we can see the beach. Now it's our turn. Men scramble to their feet, equipment is adjusted, lifebelts made more secure, for all around us artillery shells are falling and already several boats have been hit. Rifles are loaded and the safety taken off. The shore is now right off the bow. The coxswain signals me that we're about to touch down, the ramp is lowered and the Sgt. and I stepped off into four feet of water. I look behind, and the men are already off the boat and scattered for protection against the bullets which are singing around us but for the most part hitting the water. It was a hell of

---

[32] The New Tribune, Issue No. 5, 1994, Al Gibbs

[33] Newsweek, June 19, 1944: p. 73, Kenneth G. Crawford

a feeling. We had about 500 yards of water to cross, we couldn't run cause the water was too deep, we couldn't crouch, we couldn't do anything except just what we did. Wade on into shore. Finally, we made it, we were on the beach and could begin to fight back and to do our work.[34] Our work on that day would earn citations for the entire battalion, and a separate one for C Company and for A Company." While the demolitionists were blowing the obstacles, Companies A and C (Capt. Birra's company) of the 237th Engineer Combat Battalion, which had landed at H-hour, were blowing gaps in the seawall, removing wire, and clearing paths through sand dunes beyond. For these tasks the two companies had bangalore torpedoes, mine detectors, explosives, pioneer tools, and markers. Later in the morning they received equipment to bulldoze roads across the dunes. By 0930 UTAH Beach was free of all obstacles.[35]

The 70th Tank Battalion, touched down on Utah Beach at H-hour, 0630, reinforcing the 8th Infantry Regiment. A and B Companies were equipped with duplex drive amphibious tanks, commonly referred to as DD tanks. They landed in the first wave, reinforcing the 1st and 2nd Battalion respectively. C Company, not DD equipped, had four dozer blades and landed in the third wave at H plus fifteen minutes, directly on the beach from LCT's, with detachments of the 299th and 237th Engineer Combat Battalions. These engineer units also had four tank dozers. Elements of the tank battalion forward echelon followed in later waves.[36] C Company, commanded by 1st Lieutenant John L. Ahearn, landed with the engineers on both Tare Green and Uncle Red beaches. They cleared the beaches of enough obstacles to ensure unobstructed landing of troops to follow. The dozer tanks provided cover from small arms and artillery fire for the dismounted engineers while they placed charges to blow those obstacles which could not be pushed aside by the tank dozers.[37]

---

[34] Letter Home From Alfred F. Birra, July 12, 1944

[35] www.history.army.mil/html/reference/Normandy/TS/COE/COE15.htm

[36] Armor in Operation Neptune (Establishment of the Normandy Beachhead, A Research Report Prepared by Committee 10, Officers Advanced Course, The Armored School, 1948-1949, Fort Knox, Kentucky, May 1949, p. 26

[37] Armor in Operation Neptune (Establishment of the Normandy Beachhead, A Research Report Prepared by Committee 10, Officers Advanced Course, The Armored School, 1948-1949, Fort Knox, Kentucky, May 1949, p. 27

Kenneth Crawford continued, "I came across a brigadier general (Theodore Roosevelt Jr.), assistant commander of the division spear heading the attack. He was as wet as I and shivering even worse. He huddled against the wall at its higher point, wrapped in an Army blanket and sitting cross-legged, Indian-fashion. He had landed with the first wave, an innovation for brass. Two aides were trying to make his field radio work. It refused. In front of the place he sat, engineers had erected a pretentious sign proclaiming this to be General Headquarters of the beach. "That's war for you," the general complained. "The field commanders don't know where in hell their own men are, to say nothing of the enemy. They give orders anyway. It's a good thing I was here early to get that wall blown." I happen to know that the men who blew the wall had needed no orders. They came ashore knowing precisely where it was to be blown and carried the equipment to do it. Anyway, it was nice to have a general on hand so early in the game. Particularly because he had dry cigarettes, having had the forethought to wrap them in a rubber receptacle ordinarily used for quite another purpose. The general wondered what was going on at the dunes, about a mile away. I volunteered to take a look. As I stood on the dune looking, a captain called me a fool and ordered me down. He said I'd draw fire. I reported to the general that his men were already visible in the village. "I'll take a look myself," he said. He mounted the dune, stood erect, and looked. I gave the captain what I hope was a withering glance. Shortly, though, there was a whine and we all hit the dirt. For a grandfather, the general turned out to be extremely agile. The captain had the bad taste to laugh raucously. Shortly before noon the unit commanders started turning up at headquarters with their reports. Lt. Col. C. Simmons of New York, a lank man commanding one spearhead battalion (1st Battalion, 8th Regiment), reported that he had made contact by signal with the paratroopers that landed the night before H Hour in the geographical center of the Cherbourg Peninsula."[38]

Lt. Col. Conrad Simmons lived in NYC his whole life and had applied for officers training as WWI was ending. He was commissioned as an officer in late 1918 and served in the Army as a Second Lieutenant until being discharged in 1919. Knowing the war was over, but still wanting to be part of the military, Simmons enlisted in the New York National Guard in 1919 with the 51st New York Machine Gun Squadron. During this time back in

---

[38] Newsweek, June 19, 1944, p. 73, Kenneth G. Crawford

New York, he studied at Columbia University, earning a Bachelor of Science and starting up a road construction company. Eventually, the machine gun squadron was converted into the 101st New York Anti-Tank Battalion, and Simmons was named its commander. The 101st was federalized in 1941 and attached to the 8th Infantry Regiment, which was sent overseas.[39]

Meanwhile, elements of B and C Companies (70th Tank Battalion), with the C Company Commander, Lieutenant Ahearn, and the Second Battalion, Eight Infantry, commanded by Lieutenant Colonel Carlton O. MacNeely, moved south along the beach toward Pouppeville. They encountered continuous small arms fire all the way. G Company received artillery fire and ran into a mine field as well, when it approached a strongpoint at Beau Guillot. Tank fire forced the enemy in the town to capitulate. The tank-infantry team pushed on toward Exit 1. As they passed the minefield, C Company's commander saw a wounded paratrooper lying in the minefield behind the sea wall. Lt. Ahearn stopped his tank, told his crew to stay in it, dismounted to rescue the wounded man. As he was picking his way through the minefield, he tripped one or more mines which blew his feet off. His crew dismounted and, with the aid of ropes, succeeded in getting both men out of the minefield without accident. They evacuated them to the beach for return to England. 1st Lt. Dwight McKay assumed command of the company.[40]

Kenneth Crawford continued, "Toward evening I consulted a Navy beachmaster, who had set up a traffic-control station near General Headquarters, about transportation back to the mother ship. He put me on a small personnel barge. It was carrying seven wounded, including my 200 pounder, back to ship's sick bay. I provided cigarettes and water. Mistaking me for hospital corpsman, one of the boys complained bitterly about the service. He said he needed more blankets. My large friend asked me several times to see if the fingers of his broken arm were still there and, if so, to straighten them out. The 11 miles between the mother ship and the shore seemed even longer than it had that morning. Over good wardroom coffee that night and the next day we Monday-morning-quartebacked the whole operation. Veterans aboard agreed that no major amphibious undertaking they had ever seen or heard of had gone off so nearly as planned in briefing

---

[39] In France Military Death Index, 1914-1961, Family Search, Family Tree
[40] Armor in Operation, P. 28

rooms. The timing of the artillery fire and the landings had been perfect. But for the perverseness of the elements there hadn't been a hitch."[41]

Capt. Crisson continued, "One German officer had his wife with him when captured. I later ran into him on the LST where he was trying to secure a state room for her and himself. He finally went below, assured that she would be taken care of. I arrived at the aid station about 1200 which was set up in a small field left of church (Crisson would have undoubtedly seen Capt. Lucien M. Strawn, Battalion Surgeon and in fact Strawn was awarded the Silver Star for bravery during the invasion). I was evacuated on a LCT to a LST which had a hospital with Army personnel in attendance. While traveling from shore I saw quite a few small boats that had been sunk. Enemy artillery shelling of these boats was very heavy. Mine sweepers were very active as the mines kept drifting back into the channels. I remained on the LST off the beach for three or four days. In the beginning when we left the boats, we had at least 100 yards of water to wade through. We were supposed to land at 0630. I do not know exactly when we did land. We fired black smoke from a special projector attached to the boat as we approached the shore and our naval fire lifted after that signal. We fired two smoke shells. The spirit and morale of the men was fine. Even after passing what I took to be a naval patrol boat turned upside down the men continued joking and kidding each other. They had to be reminded not to expose themselves. Many of them yelled like Indians when we hit the water and, in fact, several had their hair cut (a tuft on top of head) similar to the Mohawk method of wearing their hair (faces smeared with paint). Troops were very glad they landed for the real thing and not a "dry run."[42]

Most of the enemy troops in the beach defenses surrendered with obvious relief, but there was one German officer whose strongpoint had surrendered perhaps against his will. The officer was very Prussian, stiff and haughty. An American Army photographer, who had landed with the leading elements, was taking a picture of the first German prisoners. The officer refusing to be photographed turned his back on the camera and stood at rigid attention. Just then a German shell came down. Everyone tucked except the Prussian officer. He alone was killed by the shell.[43]

---

[41] Newsweek, June 19, 1944: p. 73, Kenneth G. Crawford

[42] 8th Regiment Interview, Capt. Robert C. Crisson, Commanding Co. C, 8th Inf

[43] 8th Regiment Daily Summaries, p. 5

Snipers were a nuisance though the losses from them were not high. American soldiers went up in the church steeple to get a sniper; the space was too narrow for any more to get up. The rest of the Americans waiting outside the church heard a great commotion of yelling and shouting in the steeple, then saw a body come flying out of the belfry window. The men on the ground held their breath wondering which it would be. It was the German.[44] Lt. Col. Simmons, C.O., 1st Battalion of the 8th, said that several times they ran into a German trick of putting a German dummy in a tree with a cap pistol rigged with a string. When American soldiers approached, the German sniper concealed on the ground would pull the string firing the cap pistol. While the Americans fired at the dummy the German sniper picked them off. Every night they would comb the surrounding woods and hunt for snipers. Many snipers would be killed.[45]

In reviewing the action of the first day, the outstanding feature was the low rate of casualties in relation to the resistance which was met, and can be described to the skill, training and courage of the average soldier in the assault units. The 1st Battalion of the German 919th Regiment had occupied the beach defenses in the sector attacked by the 8th Infantry, falling back as the attack progressed. Although the enemy possessed great fire power with all types of weapons which they used to greatest advantage, their defense was not actually stubborn. Enemy morale was extremely low, evidenced by the fact that great amounts of arms and equipment was abandoned and also by the fact that captured Germans couldn't understand how the American Troops had managed to breach their defenses which their leader had declared impregnable.[46]

There were a number of cases of heroism beyond the call of duty performed by the 8th Infantrymen during the initial assault which cannot remain unrecognized. Two of the notable instances concerned Capt. Crisson and Chaplain Bruno Luechinger, the Catholic Chaplain of the 8th. Capt. Crisson led his company vigorously in the assault on enemy positions on the beach. Although painfully wounded in the leg, he continued to lead his company against the beach and inland strongpoints until the beach had been secured. Only then did he accept medical aid and allow himself to be evacuated. His vigorous leadership and extraordinary

---

[44] 8th Regiment daily Summaries, p. 6

[45] 8th Regiment Daily Summaries, p. 7

[46] 8th Regiment Daily Summaries, p. 6

bravery, despite a painful wound, and his complete disregard for his own welfare, was a material factor in the success of his company in attaining its objective. Capt. Crisson was awarded the Silver Star for his actions.[47] Chaplain Bruno Luechinger was the son of immigrants and born in New York City in 1909. His parents were born in Switzerland and Austria. He became an ordained Minister at the Catholic Archdiocese in New York and registered for the draft on October 16, 1940. He landed with the foremost assault elements of the 1st Battalion, also advanced through heavy enemy fire with the men, rendering what assistance he could, both physically and spiritually, to wounded men of all creeds and denominations, and by his great example of courage and spiritual composure, inspired the troops with greater confidence and to greater effort. Chaplain Luechinger (and Chaplain Ellenberg of the 8th) were the first Allied chaplains to land in France.[48] On D-day, total casualties amounted to only fourteen killed and sixty-three wounded. Through the precise, speedy, and marvelously efficient job done by the 8th Infantry Medical Detachment, innumerable lives were saved and the wounded were quickly evacuated by boat from the beach, some of them reaching England where they received the best possible medical attention on the evening of the same day they had been wounded.[49] Chaplain Luechinger would serve as 1st Battalion Chaplain for the entire war. Although he would remarkably survive the war, he would die in his office in the rectory of St. John's Church at a young age of 52 years old. The toll of war outlasts the battlefield.

On June 6, 1944, Capt. George G. Holochwost (29th Field Artillery, 8th Infantry Regiment) was directing cannon fire against an enemy position close to him. The enemy was wiped out but he was wounded. Although he realized he was exposed and would be wounded, Capt. Holochwost continued to direct cannon fire against the enemy. "The boys of this division really did justice to the long years of training," said Capt. Holochwost.[50] He was awarded the Silver Star, Bronze Star and Purple Heart for his valor. Another New York native, Holochwost was born in Brooklyn, New York. He received his BS at Cornell University, Class of 1937. He was a fruit and

---

[47] Silver Star Citation, Capt. Robert C. Crisson
[48] 8th Regiment Daily Summaries, p. 7
[49] 8th Regiment Daily Summaries, p. 7
[50] The Morning Herald (Uniontown, Pennsylvania) June 30, 1944

vegetable inspector before the war. He would stay in the U.S. Army until June 1967, rising to the rank of Major.

Growing up in Houston, Texas, Chester Palmer attended Rice University and worked at Humble Oil & Refinery as a Boiler-maker helper. After enlisting in the U.S. Navy on August 10, 1942, Lt. Chester L. Palmer was assigned to the U.S.S. Nevada. On D-Day, Palmer was a Navy Lieutenant assigned to Gun Fire Control Duties with the 1st Battalion, 8th Infantry, 4th Division. He recalled either being in the LCVP with Lt. Col. Simmons (Battalion Commander) or in the first wave or just behind it. As they hit the beach, he recalled generally moving to the right. He was not sure if they crossed causeway #1 or #2. Regardless, on either June 7 or 8, 1944, he was shot out of a tree near St. Mere Eglise while spotting gunfire from the Battleship Nevada. It occurred to him that he might have been taken for a sniper since he was up in a tree. On the other hand, he speculated that possibly an 88 Shell-burst fragment might have hit him in the rear-end. Whatever the case, he did not recall much after falling from the tree.[51] The U.S.S. Nevada was the only ship present at Pearl Harbor and Normandy. Disabled at Pearl Harbor, the battleship returned to active service and served with distinction in the Atlantic and in the Pacific. That service included several of the most important battles of the war including Guadalcanal, Iwo Jima and also present at Tokyo Bay when the Japanese surrendered on the U.S.S. Missouri. But the Nevada unleashed her guns on June 6, 1944. Records show she took out over 70 Panzer tanks in support of our troops.[52] During the invasion, Nevada's 10 14-inch guns battered German land fortifications and emplacements as enemy shells fell harmlessly around her and mines floated nearby, none of them striking their target. The Nevada expended 876 rounds from her main batteries and 3,500 from her five-inch guns.[53]

---

[51] 1994 IVY Leaves, p. 41

[52] The USS Nevada's role in D-Day 75 years ago, by Tom Hawley

[53] David Henley: USS Nevada supported D-Day landings 75 years ago by David C. Henley, June 5, 2019

The 70th Tank Battalion

On D Day plus two, June 8, the 70[54] Tank Battalion (A,B,C), spent the day in refitting, maintenance, and rest in the vicinity of Ste. Mere Eglise. B and C Companies were astride the road north of town where they had been at the end of action on 7 June. A Company had replaced C as reserve. They, with Battalion Headquarters elements, were in an orchard about five hundred yards northeast of town.[54]

About 1700 hours, the 70th Tank Battalion was assigned the mission of attacking enemy infantry positions in the area north and northeast of Azeville. Companies A and B attacked within their zone of action across the front of the 22nd Infantry, and Company C was placed in reserve. The path of the attack was a sweep through sparsely wooded terrain, through Azeville, and on to the northeast to describe a loop and go back past Azeville to the starting point. There was no intent to take and hold any ground, but rather to disrupt, destroy, and harass the enemy in that area to the maximum. The attack was executed in late evening to gain surprise and security for the tanks. On the way to the attack position they encountered scattered artillery fire. About 1900 an artillery round seriously wounded the C Company Commander, Lieutenant McKay. Captain Abert M. Krekler assumed command of the company. The attack was supported by artillery fire on enemy strongpoints to the front and flank. The attack started at 1930 hours and was successfully completed at 2230 hours. After this attack the battalion returned to the area they had occupied during the day.[55]

---

[54] Amor in Operation, p. 35-36

[55] Armor in Operation, p. 36

Shortly after Azeville was captured in mid-afternoon, June 9, General Barton issued an order creating a task force which that same day was to bypass Crisbecq and the other German strong points along the coastal headlands and swing northeast to "capture Quineville and the high ground west thereof." Quineville was the eastern anchor of the German defenses. The task force, which was to have first priority on division fires, consisted of the 22nd Infantry, the 899th Tank Destroyer Battalions and the 746th Tank Battalion (less detachments); it was commanded by Brig. Gen. Henry A. Barber. Led by tanks, the 22nd Infantry was to advance in a column of battalions (3d, 2d, 1st) on Ozeville, its first objective. Crisbecq was to be contained by a force of tank destroyers and infantry and was to be neutralized by division artillery at the time of the attack. The containing force, commanded by Maj. Hutson M. Betty, consisted of Company C, 22nd Infantry; Company C, 4th Engineer Combat Battalion Company C, 899th Tank Destroyer Battalion.[56] Hutson, a former starting center on the University of Missouri and Engineering School student, had enlisted in the U.S. Army on February 1, 1941 and was assigned to the 8th Infantry Regiment on Special Staff as a Special Service Officer in Field Artillery.

The task force moved out at 1630, but it was stopped by fire from strong enemy positions at the crossroads west of Chateau de Fontenay and forced to dig in for the night. For three days (10-12 June) the task force struggled with little success to overcome the enemy resistance, its right flank exposed to the bypassed enemy strong points at Crisbecg, Dangueville, Chateau de Fontenay, and Fontenay-sur- Mer and its left flank to the German positions in the gap of about a mile and a half that separated the 22nd and 12th Infantry Regiments. The task force lacked sufficient strength to protect both of its flanks and at the same time push ahead. Unfavorable weather denied it air support.[57]

---

[56] 1st Battalion, 22nd Infantry, 1-22infantry.org/history/crisbecq.htm

[57] 1st battalion, 22nd Infantry, 1-22infantry.org/history/crisbecq.htm

A Brave Chaplain Luechinger

On June 9th, in the vicinity of Fresville, France, enemy troops, employing small arms, machine gun, mortar and artillery fire, had inflicted severe casualties upon several rifle companies, shaking the morale of our attacking troops, by their unyielding defense. Chaplain Luechinger (8th Infantry Regiment, 1st Battalion) voluntarily went forward, through heavy enemy fire, to the battalion front line positions where he worked fearlessly and tirelessly in giving comfort, both spiritual and physical, to the casualties. With complete abandon, he exposed himself to enemy fire while he knelt and prayed with the wounded and dying. He assisted litter bearers in evacuating men from an area which was under simultaneous fire from hostile and friendly troops. Later Chaplain Luechinger lent active assistance in the removal of the battalion aid station to a location less subject to hostile fire. He then continued to assist the medical officers in administering to the wounded men and also ministered to their spiritual needs, retaining his composure even when the aid station was struck by enemy artillery fire. During this period, he went forward a second time and assisted litter bearers in evacuating casualties, under exposure to direct sniper fire. Chaplain Bruno Luechinger's courageous ministration and selfless concern for the wounded at this critical time were a source of inspiration to the officers and enlisted men of the battalion and elicited the deepest gratitude of the wounded men.[58] For his gallantry under fire carrying wounded men to shelter, Chaplain (Captain) Bruno Luechinger received the Silver Star Decoration with Oak Cluster for his actions on June 9, 1944. The winning of this coveted award was one phase of his military career which Chaplain Luechinger would never discuss seriously.[59]

---

[58] Silver Star Citation, Chaplain (Captain) Bruno Luechinger

[59] Tribute to Father Bruno, Father Julius Sullivan, O.F.M. Cap.

Brave Men Fall

On June 10th, following an early morning attack supported by hundreds of American Pursuit Planes and Bombers, the Regiment drove through Eccausseville to high ground just southwest of Montebourg. When the corps objective was reached, the battalions were ordered to dig in, assume a defensive position, reorganize, resupply, and allow the troops to rest. It was four days since the assault of the beach, 8th Infantry fought many bitter engagements with little sleep and little time to eat, or in any sense attend to personal discomfort.[60]

The Regiment maintained an aggressive defense line and carried out the functions of reorganization and resupply to strengthen its position, its personnel and to await a more complete consolidation of the beachhead before participating in a coordinated smash against Cherbourg. On the 10th of June, the over-strength, comprising 20 officers and 513 enlisted men, landed on the beach to replace the casualties which the Regiment had suffered in initial engagements. It was found that losses of equipment since D-Day had in some cases been heavy and in other cases light. Many of their mortars had been knocked out by enemy artillery. The reorganization and resupply of the Regiment was carried out with one battalion pulled back into reserve every three days to provide rest for its men. During this time patrols were active along the front and enemy forces in and around Montebourg maintained sporadic artillery and mortar fire upon their troops which resulted in many casualties.[61]

---

[60] 8th Regiment Daily Summaries, p. 8

[61] 8th Regiment Daily Summaries, p. 8

On the 10th of June, Captain John R. Garrabrant of 1st Battalion Headquarters (8th Infantry Regiment) was killed. Garrabrant attended North Carolina State University where for four years he was a member of the R.O.T.C. In 1941, he began active duty in the Army training at various U.S. Army bases. The battalion commander had assigned Garrabrant to take over Company C when it's commander, Captain Robert C. Crisson was injured on D-Day. Other officers had also been killed or wounded as the American forces advanced deeper into the French countryside. Garrabrant picked a four-man patrol to scout the area ahead of the company. He led three men into the woods, where the thick, shadowy growth provided limited visibility. Garrabrant was 25 feet ahead of the next man in his patrol when a machine gunner in the hedgerow and a sniper opened fire and hit him in the gut. Six weeks after the D-Day invasion, Garrabrant's family in Wilmington, N.C. received a telegram from the War Department that he had died in the invasion. Garrabrant was awarded the Distinguished Service Cross for his valor in combat. He would be buried at the Normandy American Cemetery at Colleville-sur-Mer, Normandy, France.[62]

On June 10th, 1944, Lt. Charlie H. Jones of 1st Battalion Headquarters (8th Infantry Regiment) was killed. Born in Bryant, Wisconsin, he had graduated from high school and was a stenographer and typist at the People's Bank in Antigo, Wisconsin. While serving as Battalion Intelligence Officer, 1st Lt. Charlie Jones volunteered to lead a patrol into a small village to seek out and destroy an antitank gun and a machinegun. Securing a tank for support, he led the patrol into the village. As his patrol entered the edge of the village it was suddenly pinned down by enemy small arms and machine gun fire. Locating the position of the enemy guns, despite the intense enemy fire and with complete disregard for his own safety, he moved out in front of the patrol to direct the fire of the tank. While directing the fire of the tank upon the enemy position, he was killed. Lt. Jones was awarded the Distinguished Service Cross for his valor in combat.[63]

On the same day, June 10, 1944, Capt. Gail B Lee, Commander of B Company 1st Battalion, 8th Infantry Regiment), was wounded in action during an attack on Hau de LaRiviere, France. Despite his painful wound, he refused to be evacuated. He continued to personally lead his company, completely disregarding his own safety, in the face of intense enemy fire.

---

[62] Normandy American Cemetery, abmc.nomadmobileguides.com/Normandyophp?page= narrative&id=cont-848, DSC

[63] Distinguished Service Cross Citation, Lt. Charlie H. Jones

Under his gallant leadership, his company drove the enemy from their commanding position, thereby securing the company objective. For his valor in combat, Lee was awarded the Distinguished Service Cross.[64] He also received the Bronze Star and Purple Heart. Lee, 1 of 13 children, was born in Mississippi (although some records indicate Louisiana), was raised in Walthall, Mississippi. He was a farm hand and worked on general farms. He enlisted in the National Guard in late 1940. Lee had a war time wedding with an all military twist in Pensacola, Florida on May 4, 1945. He married 2nd Lt. Enid E. Erwin, ANC, lately returned from duty in the United Kingdom, and assigned to duty at Welch Convalescent hospital in Daytona Beach. The Maid of Honor was Cpl. Margaret Erwin, WAC, sister of the bride and the bride's brother, Maj. Wallace Erwin, was best man. Lt. Erwin joined the Army Nurse corps in August 1942. She served in England, Ireland, and Scotland from September 1943, until December 1944. She had her share of robot bombs and the hospital where she was stationed in England, cared for men wounded in the invasion. Paratroopers were on their operating tables even before the infantry landed, as they were flown back to England. Captain Lee was wounded four days after landing on Utah Beach. He was evacuated to the hospital in which Lt. Erwin was serving, and it was there, that they met. Lt. Erwin and Captain Lee met in the hospital in England, they were evacuated on the same hospital ship to the United States, sent to the same general hospital, and after a brief honeymoon, both returned to Welch Convalescent hospital, where Captain Lee was also assigned. Captain Lee would stay in the U.S. Army after the war and fight in the Korean War where he became a Lt. Colonel. His service ended in Pensacola, Florida.[65]

In addition, on June 10th, 1st Lt. Richard E. Cardoze was awarded the Silver Star for the initiative and courage displayed during fighting that day.[66] He was born in Falmouth, Massachusetts and enlisted in the U.S. Army on February 2, 1942. Another soldier motivated by the Pearl Harbor attack. Prior to the war, he received 2 years of education and worked as an accountant and auditor. On June 10th, a total of 10 officers and 66 enlisted men were reported missing. The greatest number of casualties taken from enemy fire were the result of artillery adjusted for air bursts, against which there was virtually no protection.

---

[64] Distinguished Service Cross Citation, Capt. Gail B. Lee

[65] Pensacola News Journal (Pensacola, Florida) May 6, 1945

[66] Silver Star Citation, 1st Lt. Richard E. Cardoze

The Strain of War

On June 15th, 1944, 1st Lt. Gerald S. Doubler was evacuated due to exhaustion.[67] It is not known if he returned to duty but his service release date was September 21, 1944. Born in Warren, Illinois, Doubler graduated from Warren High School and was associated with his father and brothers in farming. He volunteered for service in the Army. According to family, he never spoke of the war. The horrors of war were undoubtedly a lifelong burden for many soldiers. He never left Warren and is buried in Warren, Illinois.

In June or perhaps later in 1944, 1st Lt. Robert E. Ertmer was also evacuated most likely due to exhaustion.[68] It is not known where Ertmer served afterward but his service release date was December 11, 1945. Ertmer was born in Mitchell, South Dakota. His family moved to Illinois. After graduating from Aguin High School, Ertmer was manager at Krogull Junior Market in Stephenson, Illinois. He enlisted in the U.S. Army on March 5, 1941. He married Miss Alice Mary LaGrand on September 15, 1942 in the Eight Infantry Chapel at Camp Gordon, August, Georgia. The Eighth Infantry Regimental flag and the American flag also stood at the altar. The bride entered the chapel on the arm of Col. John Van Fleet. Officers of the Eighth Infantry and their wives attended the ceremony. At the time, Ertmer was stationed with Company B, First Battalion, Eighth Infantry at Camp Gordon, Augusta, Georgia. He is buried in Wheat Ridge, Colorado. His grave indicates he was a 1st Lt., 4th Infantry Division.

---

[67] 8th Regiment Daily Summaries

[68] Capt. Max Barrick document

A Sniper Strikes

Ralph Lester Thomas was born in Beaufort, North Carolina. He was a graduate of the Oak Ridge Military Institute and the University of Tennessee. He enlisted in the U.S. Army in 1940 and was assigned to the 8th Infantry Regiment, 1st Battalion Staff. On the 23rd of June, Capt. Ralph Thomas was standing behind a tree organizing some small arms fire when a German sniper shot his left elbow. He was sent to a hospital England for six weeks. He was eventually reunited with his battalion.[69] He would go on to earn a Silver Star, Bronze Star and Purple Heart.

---

[69] Ralph L. Thomas personal recollection

A Leader Falls

On the 24th of June, Attacks were made against strongly fortified German positions 1100 yards east of La Glaciers, France, consisting of a maze of tunnels, dugouts, and gun emplacements which boasted an amazing amount of fire power. The enemy continued a stubborn defense on strong points in the Cherbourg Sector, but by this time, desperate and fully realizing the inevitability of their defeat, came out of their holes and fortifications when surrounded or in peril of annihilation. It was estimated that at this time enemy strength consisted of 2000 combat soldiers capable of being reinforced by service troops, labor battalions and if the situation became too critical, every available male of fighting age within the city, regardless of nationality or extent of military training.[70] At least 100 P-47's dropped 24 1,000 lb. bombs on strongpoints in front of the 1st Battalion; 23 bombs hit the target. Immediately the enemy troops came out of the fortifications and started running across the fields, where they were slaughtered by mortar fire. The strongpoint, which had been a tough nut on the previous day, was taken without further trouble.[71] The 8th Regiment resumed the attack, sending the 1st Battalion forward, which reached its objective at 1300 on the 24th of June. As the attack advanced, resistance was met from automatic weapons which had survived the initial preparation, but which were quickly and effectively overcome. The attack continued aggressively to the north and having reduced several German strong points, arrived on high ground, where the 2nd Battalion dug in. The 3rd Battalion, held in reserve

---

[70] 8th Regiment Daily Summaries, p. 12

[71] 8th Regiment Interviews Note on Battle for Cherbourg

during the attack sent a strong patrol made up of an entire company to coordinate its operation with the 2nd Battalion along the front. The 1st Battalion later advanced under extremely heavy enemy artillery fire to the northwest.[72] 2nd Lt. Ray W. Sherman was killed. About 1800, Lt. Col. Simmons was killed by a direct hit on his foxhole. A total of 6 Battalion commanders out of 10 were lost, 4 of them killed. A counter-attack launched against the 8th Infantry shortly before 1800 was repulsed by use of tanks and all division artillery. The 8th called, as counterattack developed and Col. Simmons was killed, and asked for increased artillery fire. Objections were raised. General Barton was present at the time and he grabbed the phone. "This is Barton. I want all of the artillery I've got to fire on….." In a few minutes all of the artillery came down.[73] The counter attack was repulsed. Lt. Col. Simmons had constantly distinguished himself by extraordinary heroism and brilliant tactical performance since the assault of the beach on June 6th. He had been a wonderful leader of troops, embodying all the characteristics of bravery, gallantry, consideration for his men and an utter refusal to subject them to any of the dangers and hardships of battle which he did not himself experience as every day routine.[74]

---

[72] 8th Regiment Daily Summaries, p. 13

[73] 8th Regiment Interview Note on Battle for Cherbourg

[74] 8th Regiment Daily Summaries, p. 13

A Tank Battle

Born in West Elkton, Ohio, Albert M. Krekler graduated from Indiana University. Afterward he moved to Clinton, Indiana. He enlisted in the U.S. Army and was assigned to the 70th Tank Battalion. Captain Albert M. Krekler was the C Company Tank commander since June 8, 1944. On July 15, 1944, when five of his tanks were disabled and burned by intense enemy tank fire, Capt. Krekler disregarded the grave risk involved by going forward on foot in the face of fierce fire to each tank and assisted the wounded men who were unable to get out. When he had placed his men in comparative safety, he courageously returned to the forward position, still on foot and under concentrated enemy fire, in order to locate the enemy tanks and bring artillery fire upon them. In doing so he was wounded by shell-fire but refused to be evacuated until his men were properly cared for. For his valor on this day, Capt. Krekler was awarded the Silver Star.[75] He would be wounded five times before the war was over earning a Bronze Star and Purple Heart (five clusters). The 70th Tank Battalion would later be awarded the Distinguished Unit Citation for its action on D-Day.

---

[75] The Daily Clintonian, December 20, 1944

Captain Crisson and Hemingway

Around mid-July, 1944, Capt. Crisson met Ernest Hemingway. Crisson knew Hemingway's brother, who was the Division photographer. When Crisson was hurt in the stomach, the Division Surgeon was brought in to treat him near the front (Colonel Barton's reasoning was that Crisson would "go AWOL anyway!") Crisson was eventually moved back to the Division to recover. He found a hayloft in a barn and set up a sleeping bag. Hemingway's brother set up his sleeping bag next to Crisson. Crisson had read "For Whom the Bell Tolls" and was impressed, his brother said it was difficult for Hemingway to write. He would work for several days on small passages.[76]

According to Crisson, Ernest Hemingway was generally a pest, always having to prove how brave he was and drawing fire. People would say, "Damn Ernie, get down!" Hemingway spent his whole life trying to prove he was courageous. In Percy, Normandy, Hemingway asked around where he could find Crisson. The objective was to take the town of Percy, which lay at the end of a long highway and to capture all of the Germans in the town. Crisson decided to cut the Germans off by swinging around to the back of the town. Normally an element would be kept in the front, advancing towards the town, while another would be sent around back but they only had about 500 troops. Therefore, the entire force swung around back with no one out in front. Hemingway decided to follow the troops to Percy. He got right in his jeep, going straight down the highway towards the front of the town. The Germans had already pulled out of the town but none of

---

[76] Megan Snow Notes on Ernest Hemingway, April 8, 2007

the Americans had arrived yet. Hemingway found some local Frenchmen and demanded to know where the Germans and Americans were. He was directed to some Germans hiding in a basement. He demanded they come out, and when they did not, he threw in a hand grenade. Three or four Germans came out of the basement, Hemingway took them prisoner and brought them to Crisson. Crisson said, "Where have you been?" Hemingway just laughed. Hemingway was always laughing. In fact, the last time Crisson saw Hemingway was after taking Paris. Two assault companies were fighting north of the city. The command post was totally exposed, bullets were flying. Crisson was lying on his back clinging to the radio and he looked up and saw Hemingway above him grinning. Crisson said, "Get your ass down!" Hemingway responded, "I'm okay, Bob!" Crisson didn't admire it, it was generally a bother and detrimental to the mission to have unnecessary exposure.[77]

On the 20th of July, the regiment assembled at 1400 for presentation of awards by General Barton to men who had distinguished themselves in former engagements. Among those awarded the Silver Star were the Regimental Commander, Colonel James S. Rodwell; Lt Col John H Meyer, Major Fred W. Collins, and Major George L. Mabry. Jr. Towards evening, the Regiment prepared to again move up to the lines.[78]

---

[77] Megan Snow Notes on Ernest Hemingway, April 8, 2007
[78] 8th Regiment Daily Summaries, p. 16

The Thrust South

On the 21st of July, the Regiment moved from LE COMPTE just south-east of CARETAN to an assembly area south of ST JEAN DE DAYE to prepare for a thrust toward the south into enemy territory in conjunction with the 3rd Armored Division. The drive, tremendous in scope, was scheduled to be perhaps of greater magnitude than the initial assault of the Normandy beaches. Its potentialities were boundless. This campaign, effectively concentrating all types of personnel and equipment on the Normandy beachhead into a channel of offensive action, might well strike a blow against the enemy which would prove the decisive battle resulting in a quick defeat of the Third Reich. As the 8th Infantry moved into its assembly areas behind the proposed line of departure, hardened, battle weary men of the Regiment were once more ready to close with the enemy in hand to hand combat if necessary and drive him from his foxhole with the cold steel blade which he feared more than bombs and artillery. While Infantrymen had received little rest since the assault on the Normandy beaches on D-Day, prolonged periods of relaxation were now of little use to them. They were keyed up to the extent that they had to keep going. By this time the Regiment had participated in more days of unbroken fighting than any other Infantry Regiment which had landed in France on June 6th. 8th Infantryman were grimly determined to make their long, hard won days of combat experience pay off in greater slaughter among the Germans than the Russians had precipitated at STALENGRAD and SEVASTOPOL.[79]

---

[79] 8th Regiment Daily Summaries, p. 16

On the 22nd of July, Battalion Commanders made a reconnaissance of routes forward from the assembly area to the line of departure and prepared their men and equipment for an attack at H-hour on D-day, the time of which had not yet been designated. Plans were drawn up for an attack coordinating tanks, air corps and infantry, and after the final picture had been thoroughly discussed and revised, necessary contacts were made with supporting units and with the 30th Division which would attack on their left, and with the 9th Division which would attack on their right. Heavy rains on the following day delayed the zero hour by making effective air support impossible. Thus H-hour was again postponed by elements which the foot sloggers cursed without restraint.[80]

Early on the morning of July 24th, the Regiment was notified that H-hour would be at 1300. Colonel Rodwell held a staff meeting of Battalion and Company Commanders at 0900 at which time he gave the order for the attack and last-minute instructions. When the staff officers and unit commanders returned to their organizations, they were received with the greatest display of enthusiasm and thirst for battle which had ever been witnessed in the ranks of the 8th Infantry. The troops in the line impatiently awaited H-hour and the opportunity to hurl the Germans in their sector back through Normandy with increasing momentum. The mission of the 8th Infantry with its attached units (Co A and Co C, 4th Engineer Battalion, Co B, 87th Chemical Battalion, 634th Tank Destroyer Battalion, the 70th Tank battalion, and the 4th Division Artillery) was to pass through the 39th Infantry Regiment of the 9th Division, and, supported by dive bombers, medium bombers and heavies, drive through the bombed areas, seize the objective, protect the gap between Marigny and St Jules and advance to within 500 yards of the Pierre-St Lo highway. The 8th Infantry would then continue the advance, employing artillery, mortar, tank and bomb support. In this, one of the largest operations of coordinated forces in the Second World War, the 8th Infantry would spearhead the drive, clearing paths for other troops to follow.[81]

The Regiment was opposed by elements of the 14th Parachute Regiment, the Second Reconnaissance Parachute Battalion, and units of the 901st Panzer Regiment. These troops, composed of first-class fighting men most of whom were fanatical Nazis, had manned a series of strategic strong points

---

[80] 8th Regiment Daily Summaries, p. 16
[81] 8th Regiment Daily Summaries, p. 16

around houses, along hedgerows and on high ground which were supported by tanks and self-propelled guns. Dive bombing along a line just south of the Pierre-St Lo highway, started at H plus 25 minutes and was resumed again a short time later. Mucky weather cancelled the heavy bombing, yet since the bombing mission had been already partially completed, the Regiment attacked as previously planned with the restriction that it would not cross the Pierres-St Lo highway. The attack progressed speedily under heavy artillery and mortar fire, and by 1414 the 2nd Battalion which had been the leading Battalion, had reached a position 100 yards north of the highway with Companies "G" and "F" abreast. At 1630, the battalion was ordered to withdraw to the best possible defenses positions where it dug in for the night. The 1st and 3rd Battalions occupied positions to the rear.[82]

The 4th Infantry Division had landed, moved inland, and turned toward the south and fought perhaps the most savage battles of the war, slugged the enemy back foot by foot, hedgerow after hedgerow, in the Periers, Carentan sector. It was then that the "Breakthrough" came. Up until this great moment we had realized what might, in a great strategic plan, be called limited objectives: a beachhead and a port through which to supply future operations. The Allied Command realized that we were advancing but that the gains were bought at such a cost as to make this virtually a war of attrition. Some great blow had to be dealt the German Army that would send it reeling back and that would give the Command the opportunity to utilize the tremendous forces which it had at its disposal and which it was amassing behind the Allied lines.[83]

It is doubtful if at this time the Germans were at all certain that there would not be landings at other points along the coast of France. Von Kluge (commander of the German Seventh Army) was planning for this. For almost a week the troops chomped at the bit expecting to be told at any moment, "This is it, boys, go to it." In preparation for the breakthrough, the Air Corps was to bombard the enemy front lines so as to destroy his ability to defend against our ensuing attack. From day to day this attack was delayed because of the weather until July 24th when a large number of planes did fly over and bombed the enemy lines. At the last minute the

---

[82] 8th Regiment Daily Summaries, p. 17

[83] 8th Regiment Daily Summaries, Breakthrough, p. 1

attack was called off when the field commanders were informed that this was not the expected preparation bombardment.[84]

On July 25th the planes again flew over, not as before or an abortive attack, but in full strength. A gigantic force of combined forces including heavy bombers, making a grand total of three thousand planes pounded the front lines. This was not just a great bombardment; it was by all odds the greatest air attack in history.[85]

Capt. Robert C. Crisson, had been wounded on D-day and evacuated to a hospital in England. He had led his men through a blanket of enemy gunfire at H-Hour and didn't stop until a piece of jagged shrapnel dug into his left leg. "They told me at the hospital I'd rejoin my old outfit after a couple of months but I didn't believe them, so one day I took off, went down to a port, and bummed a ride from an LST commander," Crisson said. Crisson's goal was to find the command post of his old outfit. Kenneth Crawford continued, "The battalion command post was set up in a windowless but still comfortable Norman farmhouse when I joined it on the eve of the big push to cut the St. Lo-Pierrers Highway. Capt. Bob Crisson, wearing a black mustache, leaning on a heavy cane, and looking twice his 23 years, came to the door followed by a pet baby donkey about the size of a full-grown Saint Bernard. It was the first time I had seen Crisson since we landed on the beach together on D Day. He had been hit twice in the leg about an hour after I left him that day and had only recently returned to active duty. He had gone AWOL from the hospital to hasten his return. One of his friends told me the story.[86]

"He walked into Division CP and reported to the old man. The old man was working and didn't look up. 'You're AWOL, Crisson.' 'Yes sir.' 'That's a serious offense.' Bob was wilting fast. Then the general looked up and said: 'I'm proud of you. Go back to your outfit.'"[87]

So, Crisson was back in France and on July 25th, Captain Robert C. Crisson, 3rd Battalion S-3, assumed command of a task force comprising Company "L", a section of heavy machine guns and part of the 3rd Battalion

---

[84] 8th Regiment Daily Summaries, Breakthrough, p. 1

[85] 8th Regiment Daily Summaries, Breakthrough, p. 1

[86] Newsweek, August 7, 1944, Kenneth G. Crawford

[87] Newsweek, August 7, 1944, Kenneth G. Crawford

CP Group. The mission of this force was to push forward and reach an objective south of the PIERRES-ST LO highway before daylight.[88]

At 0940 the first dive bombers flew over to begin the aerial attack, following them the heavy bombers. It was a magnificent sight and the Line of Departure for our troops had been a line 1000 yards behind the nearest end of the target. However, the elements intervened and as successive waves of bombers flew over dropping their bombs a huge cloud of dust formed over the target. The next formation of planes began bombing this dust cloud which consequently was considered as a target marker. Unfortunately, a wind arose and began to blow this great dust cloud back toward the 8th Infantry. As the cloud approached our front lines so did the bombs. By 1015 the cloud was actually over our line of departure and all four of the companies were being hit by bombs. Company C had only two casualties, but Company B had many men wounded and some killed. There were others that were completely stunned.[89]

Captain Crisson (Executive Officer of the 3rd Battalion) was an eyewitness of the bombardment and gave his experience. "When the big bomb exploded 30 feet from me, I was flat in a ditch beside the road. I can remember looking up after the explosion and seeing dirt and rocks raining down all around me. When I got up, I was half out of my senses. The Captain jumped up and ran over to put out a blaze in the next field, so it wouldn't "attract the bombers." That's the way it affects you. You're not rational. Many of the men were out of their heads in somewhat the same way as I was, but some of them for a much longer time. We found them just wandering around and unable to understand clearly when you spoke to them."[90]

As Captain Crisson and his men advanced in the early morning, they sighted six German tanks and about 100 enemy infantrymen on the road in front of them. Contact was instantaneous and heavy machine gun fire, 88's and rocket shells immediately were directed on positions occupied by our troops. Sensing the seriousness of the situation, Captain Crisson accompanied by three enlisted men attempted to move to the flank of the enemy to get an estimate of the situation. However, his maneuver was observed and immediately the party was subjected to direct fire which

---

[88] 8th Regiment Daily Summaries, p. 20

[89] 8th Regiment Daily Summaries, p. 2

[90] 8th Regiment Daily Summaries, p. 3

caused several casualties. With utter disregard for his own personal safety, Captain Crisson kept moving along a hedgerow to a more advantageous position. Upon reaching a "break" in the hedgerow he came face to face with a force of three Germans. The Germans, intent upon killing their lone opponent without giving away their positions to the rest of the American troops in the vicinity, struck, using their weapons as clubs. Captain Crisson fired several shots into the group, killing two, and using his rifle very advantageously, disposed of his lone opponent with a quick, straight butt stroke. Realizing the need for reinforcements and the danger of having a whole Company annihilated should the enemy realize the strength of his force, Captain Crisson ran and crawled several hundred yards back into German territory to get out of the fire that was being directed at him. Upon reaching cover, he started working his way back toward his own lines. Several enemy patrols were active in the area which necessitated skillful and tactful movements to avoid delay or capture. A short time later he returned to his men with information which enabled Company "L" to go on to the objective with little further harassment.[91] Capt. Crisson was awarded the Distinguished Service Cross for his valor. Later, Capt. Crisson offered additional details on what happened. Capt. Crisson, "I moved out behind a hedgerow, came around a corner of it and bumped into several Germans (above gives details of this encounter). I then moved farther to the flank with the idea of getting around behind the Germans, of getting back to battalion, and of bringing up resistance. I am not clear just what direction I followed. I got entirely away from the company and completely lost. My compass did not work so I just kept going. I actually went a mile and a half or more to the northeast and somewhere south of St Gilles I found some elements of the 2nd AD. I tried to get some help from them, told them I had an isolated company back there about to be annihilated by German infantry and tanks. They said, "We are sorry Bud but we have a mission of our own. We can't help you." Then I caught a jeep ride to St. Gilles, walked west down the highway to within a mile of Marigny, then turned back north and east and found the battalion CP."[92]

On July 26th, the 4th Infantry Division continued the advance to the south against continuous but disorganized resistance. The P47's worked right in front of them all day, strafing and firing their rockets sometimes

---

[91] 8th Regiment Daily Summaries, p. 20

[92] 8th Regiment Interviews, p. 15, 3rd Bn. 8th Inf Reg

50 to 75 yards in front of their lines. Never once did they hit them. It was beautiful work and very effective, especially the rockets. By late afternoon, they reached le Mesnil-Amey.[93] Many Germans were captured. During the fighting, Capt Crisson engaged a German and quickly killed him. He noticed the cap the German was wearing. "It was a patch from the Jerry cap. I suppose it made them feel more fierce to wear those things. It does no more than disgust us. This guy didn't look so fierce. Cringed in his hole like a field mouse when things got too hot and too close for him. He died like the rat he was."[94] It was now getting dark and they were approximately on the battalion objective where they wanted to stabilize for the night. But after dark orders were received to push on ahead that night to the division objective on the hill two miles farther south. Time was pressing and they could not delay to orient company commanders and work out a careful plan of advance. The roads they had to follow were small, winding, and very confusing, even on the map. In the dark officers could not use their maps anyway. They could not put out advance guards and flank guards and have any hope of maintaining control. Besides, the success of this movement would depend on slipping thru. If they got into a fight in the dark there was little chance that they would reach the objective that night.[95]

It was therefore decided to form the whole battalion in a road column and march right thru in silence. Capt. Crisson got down in a ditch with a map and memorized the route as best he could. Then the companies reorganized along the Coutances highway and started the march in column in the order, L, OP group, K and I. Radio silence was imposed to maintain secrecy; therefore, in order to keep communications with Battalion CP at Mesnil-Amey, a wire team marched with the OP group laying wire as they went.[96]

The march proceeded without any trouble for about a half mile beyond the highway. Then the wire team ran out of wire and stopped. The rest of the battalion behind them was stopped while the head of the column kept going. About a half mile farther they discovered up in front that they had only Company L and a part of the OP group and a section of machine guns. They had no A-T guns and they couldn't bring them up because of

---

[93] 8th Regiment Interviews, p. 11, 3rd Bn. 8th Inf Reg

[94] Capt. Robert Crisson Short Letter

[95] 8th Regiment Interviews, p. 11, 3rd Bn. 8th Inf Reg

[96] 8th Regiment Interviews, p. 11-12, 3rd Bn. 8th Inf Reg

the noise. Nevertheless, there was nothing to do but keep going. They went a few hundred yards to a road juncture and halted the column while two 3-men patrols were sent out both ways on the cross road. The patrol that went south never returned. They were captured, taken to Cenilly where they were released when the 2ⁿᵈ AD went thru that town, and eventually returned to us. It was very fortunate that these three men did not talk. If they had given away their situation to the enemy that night it would have been bad for them.[97]

The patrol that went to the north returned after a while with the report that the road was clear in that direction. But right behind them a German patrol of two men came down the road and passed right by the head of their column which was standing in the narrow trail where it joined the road, without seeing them, and went on to the south.[98]

Capt. Crisson, who had been leading the column and in command of this forward element, decided that it was time to hide out in the field and await the arrival of the rest of the battalion. They were now within 600 or 800 yards of a hilltop which was the objective. Captain Crisson called Capt. Dorrie and, commander of Company L, and Capt. Hill, Exec of Company L, they put their heads under a raincoat and by flashlight Captain Crisson showed them their position on the map and pointed out the field into which they should lead the company intending to get them well off the road. Capt. Crisson then went back to try to contact the remainder of the battalion which he thought would be coming up. But he could not find them and returned to L Company. In fact, the battalion never arrived that night having gotten into a tank fight farther back[99].

Meanwhile, Capt. Dorrie had led his company off the road into a field, over the next hedgerow, then turned right thru a gate into a larger field. This he thought had taken him well away from the road. In fact, the road made a bend and the field into which Company L had gone was bounded by the road on two sides. In the dark the company did not know this. Orders were issued to do no digging in order not to give their position away to the enemy. The men just sat down with their backs to the hedgerow all around the field, leaned back, and tried to get some sleep for the hour or

---

[97] 8ᵗʰ Regiment Interviews, p. 12, 3ʳᵈ Bn 8ᵗʰ Inf Reg

[98] 8ᵗʰ Regiment Interviews, p. 12, 3ʳᵈ Bn. 8ᵗʰ Inf Reg

[99] 8ᵗʰ Regiment Interviews, p. 13, 3ʳᵈ Bn. 8ᵗʰ Inf Reg

two of darkness that remained. It was raining, and everyone covered up as best he could. Capt. Hill and Capt. Crisson had thrown a German gas cape over their heads.[100]

It was about the half light of dawn, probably around 0500, when they were awakened by tanks coming down the road. The machine gunner at the north corner of the field looking up the road let the tanks go by which was the proper thing to do. When behind the tanks he saw a column of Germany infantry. That was too much for his nerves and he opened up on them with a long burst. With that everyone started shooting. The first thing Capt. Hill and Capt. Crisson remembered as they awoke under their gas cape was the firing and Capt. Dorrie running across the field and yelling cease firing. They all knew that American armor columns were due to come thru that road and captain Dorrie thought their men had started firing on their own tanks. The firing ceased and there was a sudden stillness. In that silence they could hear the jabber of Germans shouting excitedly to each other and with that the firing broke out again. From then on it was wild confusion.[101]

The German tanks (six) were now along the road on two sides of the field Crisson and L Company were in and they swung their guns in toward the field and poured everything they had on them. But the Germans were evidently as confused as we were, it was still only half light and they were just shooting wild into the field. The German infantry (about 100 men) farther north turned to their left and advanced into the first field north of L Company. "They put a sheet of tracer fire across and into our position," Crisson said. "Some sort of aerial bombs and 88's was fired into every field. It was hell. Some of the men played dead because they were right in front of the tanks that were firing over the road bank. Jerries actually crawled up and used these men for cover and rested rifles across their bodies." Crisson's men who were in the field next to that ran back into the orchard and around behind the next hedgerow. Other German infantry stopped in the road along the edge of the main field and stuck their rifles thru the bushes of the hedge and blazed away into the field. That was when Crisson's men found there was no dirt bank there. The Germans were just shooting wild. Some of our men who were lying along that ledge woke up

---

[100] 8th Regiment Interviews, p. 13, 3rd B. 8th Inf Reg

[101] 8th Regiment Interviews, p. 14, 3rd Bn. 8th Inf Reg

to see the barrels of German rifles sticking thru the bushes right above them and firing over their bodies. They just lay there and played dead. The company runners and some other men laid flat near them beside the hedgerow. These men were told to get up and get in firing position. Just as they stood up a tank shell hit the top of the hedgerow right beside them and killed two. Then a second shell hit the hedgerow and killed another. The men were led out of the direct fire and led to get around the German column. They then moved back down the road but when they returned to the original company position the Germans were all gone.[102]

---

[102] 8th Regiment Interviews, p. 14, 3rd Bn. 8th Inf Reg

Captain Strawn and Ernie Pyle

Dr. Lucien Martin Strawn was born in Uniontown, Pennsylvania. His parents moved to Morgantown, West Virginia where Strawn attended West Virginia University. After getting married in 1937 to Miss Joy Makinson. They moved to Pittsburg, Pennsylvania where Strawn worked at the Pittsburgh Medical Center. Strawn registered for the draft on October 1, 1940 and landed on Utah Beach with the 1st Battalion, 8th Infantry Regiment, as the Battalion Surgeon. Strawn would be awarded the Silver Star for bravery in action against the enemy in France.[103] Famed war correspondent, Ernie Pyle, recalled an encounter with Captain Strawn in August 1944, "One afternoon I went with our battalion medics to pick up wounded men who had been carried back to some shattered houses just behind our lines, and to gather some others right off the battlefield. The battalion surgeon was Capt. Lucien Strawn, from Morgantown, West Virginia. He drives his jeep himself and goes right into the lines with his aidmen. We drive forward about a mile in our two jeeps, so loaded with litter bearers they were even riding on the hood. Finally, we had to stop and wait until a bulldozer filled a new shell crater in the middle of the road. We had gone only about a hundred yards beyond the crater when we ran into some infantry. They stopped us and said: "Be careful where you're going. The Germans are only 200 yards up the road." Captain Strawn said he couldn't get to the wounded men that way so he turned around to try another way.

---

[103] Morning Herald, July 13, 1944

A side road led off at an angle from a shattered village we had just passed through. He decided to try to get up that road."[104]

Pyle continued, "But when we got there the road had a house blown across it, and it was blocked. We went forward a little on foot and found two deep bomb craters, also impassable. So, Captain Strawn walked back to the bulldozer, and asked the driver if he would go ahead of us and clear the road. The first thing the driver asked was, "How close to the front is it?" The doctor said, "Well, at least it isn't any closer than you are right now." So, the dozer driver agreed to clear the road ahead of us. While we were waiting a soldier came over and showed us two eggs he had just found in the backyard of a jumbled house. There wasn't an untouched house left standing in the town, and some of the houses were still smoking inside. At the far edge of the town we came to a partly wrecked farmhouse that had two Germans in it, one was wounded and the other was just staying with him. We ran our jeep into the yard and the litter bearers went on across the field. The doctor took his scissors and began cutting his clothes open to see if he was wounded anywhere except in the arm. He wasn't. But he had been sick in his stomach and then rolled over. He was sure a superman sad sack."[105]

In another incident in August, famed war correspondent Ernie Pyle recalled a moment with Capt. Lucien Strawn, "The doctor and I sat a while on the stairway inside the farmhouse, for shells had started hitting just outside again. But in a little bit the doctor got up and said he was going to see how the stretcher party was getting along. I said I'd like to go with him. He said o.k. We struck out across a sloping wheatfield. It was full of huge craters left by our bombings. There was a lull in the shelling as we crossed the field, but the trouble with lulls is that they will suddenly come to an end. As we picked our way among the craters I thought I heard, very faintly, somebody call "Help!" It's odd how things strike you in wartime. I remember thinking to myself, "Oh, pooh. That would be too dramatic, just like a book. You're just imagining it." But the doctor stopped and he said, "Did you hear somebody yelling?" So, we listened again, and this time we could hear it plainly. It seemed to come from a far corner of the field, so we picked our way over in that direction. Finally, we saw him, a soldier lying on his back near a hedgerow, still yelling "Help!" as we approached. The

---

[104] Ernie Pyle, Brave Medics Carry on Under Heavy Nazi Shelling, 8-31-1944
[105] Ernie Pyle, Brave Medics Carry on Under Heavy Nazi Shelling, 8-31-1944

aidmen who had started ahead of us had got down in a bomb crater when the shelling started, so the doctor now waved them to come on."[106]

"The wounded soldier was making an awful fuss. He was twisting and squirming, and moaning "Oh, my God! Oh, my God." He had a bandage on his right hand and there was blood on his left leg. The doctor took his scissors and cut the legging off, then cut the laces on the shoe and then peeled off a bloody sock and cut the pants leg up so he could see the wound. The soldier kept his eyes shut and kept squirming and moaning. When the doctor would try to talk to him, he would just groan and say, "Oh, my God!" Finally, the doctor got out of him that he had had a small wound in his hand and his sergeant had bandaged it and told him to start to the rear. Then, coming across the field, a shell fragment had got him in the leg. The doctor looked him over thoroughly. There were two small holes just above the ankle. The doctor said they hadn't touched the bone. I think the doctor was disgusted, He said," He's making a hell of a fuss over nothing." Then to one of the aidmen he said, "Better give him a shot of morphine to quiet him." Whereupon the soldier squirmed and moaned, "Oh, no, no, no, Oh my God!" But the doctor said go ahead and the aidman cut his sleeve up to the shoulder, stuck the needle in an squeezed the vial. The aidman, trying to be sympathetic, said to the soldier, "It's the same old needle, ain't it?" But the soldier just groaned again and said, "Oh my God!" Then one set of the litterbearers started back with our new man, and the rest of us went on to hunt for other wounded."[107]

---

[106] Ernie Pyle, Salisbury Times (Salisbury, Maryland), Wounds Disgust Some Soldiers, 8/17/1944

[107] Ernie Pyle, Salisbury Times (Salisbury, Maryland), Wounds Disgust Some Soldiers, 8/17/1944

Captain Crisson in Paris

In a letter to his mother, Capt. Crisson described the French reaction to the 4th Infantry Division in Paris, "As you must have read in the papers, the 4th Division was the first in Paris. I will never forget that day. There is no way for me to describe the joy those people showed on their faces. It is absolutely unbelievable that people could express their feelings so openly. In many sections of the place I have driven in my jeep and would find myself to be the first American there in years, women would come out crying and laughing, throwing flowers and showering you with kisses. Even old men would kiss my hand. You would feel like a God. And it was that way for every soldier. Crowds would line the streets for miles and when you started pass them, your jeep would be loaded with flowers and eats. And the girls, the most beautiful you have ever seen. Not like the wooden shoe clad people of Normandy. As we neared Paris (and this is the truth, so help me), the girls got prettier by the mile, or kilometer, as they say over here. Fred (Major Collins) is shy anyway, and you should have seen him when an old man with a long beard came up and actually kissed him. The men sure got a laugh out of that. One day when we liberated a particular town, I made the mistake of kissing a cute little girl that reminded me of Betty Jean. Well, there must have been about 50 babies in the crowd and I had to kiss every one of them. Some of the ladies even ran back into the houses to get some more babies that they had been unable to bring out before. They stick flowers in your helmet 'till you look like a walking sunflower or something. Of course, you can't go on fighting with that stuff, so we keep it politely 'til we get out of town and then have to toss them aside. This is something that I had never anticipated. As one of the boys said, "you'd better appreciate these bouquets of flowers now, for when we get in Germany, they'll have hand-grenades in them." Of course, we all had a laugh out of that and one of the men said, "Hell, when I get to Germany, I don't give a damn what they throw." What a bunch of boys to have around you!!! They'd laugh if they knew that in the next minute a whole Ranger division was coming in on them. I know because we've experienced it many times. That is why we have never yielded a yard of ground, with a spirit like that, you can't lose."[108]

In the same letter to his mother, Crisson described a few encounters with captured German soldiers, "One day I was searching a prisoner and in his pocket was a small gold chain. I think he was afraid I was going to keep it. His knees were shaking anyway because he was so scared. He said, "that from mama." I said, "From mama? Okay, you keep." I hadn't shaved for about three days and was really dirty all over. His knees stopped shaking and his faced beamed with both surprise and appreciation. I would have killed him a few minutes before his capture, even though I would not deprive him of a gift from his mother. One day we had a little Jerry that was only a kid. He spoke a little English and was very indignant. I was in a bad mood anyway, so I told him, "Boy you should be at home with your mother, you're no soldier!" And then I'd point to one of my big strapping Rangers, "As a matter of fact, I'm going to spank you," and I did. I turned him over my knee and spanked him hard. Well, he was the most hurt thing you have ever seen. I have never seen anyone so humiliated and I have never seen anyone become so humble so sudden. He began to cry and suddenly realized that he was not the Superman that Hitler had so falsely made him believe. I think he was 17 or 18 years old with the complexion of that like a baby."[109]

---

[108] Capt. Robert Crisson Letter Home, Megan Snow
[109] Capt. Robert Crisson Letter Hone, Megan Snow

A Soldier Falls

On September 19th, the 8th Infantry again maintained an aggressive defense line, maintaining constant pressure against enemy units of the Kuhne combat team, SS Das Reich and Hitler Jugend Divisions which defended their fortifications, using heavy artillery and rocket fires. The 8th Infantry, in maintaining its defense lines, awaiting the jockeying of other units in this and other sectors into a more favorable position for a final, potential thrust past the Seigfried Line. It was hoped that the allied airborne landing in Holland would enable the British, Canadian and American troops to quickly outflank the Seigfried Line and thrust defeat of Hitler's armies deep into the center of German heavy industry which might precipitate the final defeat of Hitler's armies.[110]

During the night of the 19th, and early morning of the 20th, while the Kuhne combat team remained in defensive position, the 1st battalion of the Deutschland Regiment organized a heavy counter-attack against the Regimental Sector. The second company of this battalion, which had penetrated 8th Infantry lines, later withdrew, leaving behind a small covering force which was soon annihilated.[111] In was in this engagement that 2nd Lt. Edward H Buckles stepped on a mine and was killed. He had come ashore on D-Day and fought his way through France only

---

[110] 8th Regiment Daily Summaries, p. 12
[111] 8th Regiment Daily Summaries, p. 12

56

to be killed as they began the Germany offensive. Originally born in Kansas City, Missouri, he moved to Long Beach, California where he worked nearby at the U.S. Navy on Terminal Island in San Pedro as a cost inspector of Bethlehem Steel. He had married Miss Patricia C Parmenter on May 19, 1942 and enlisted in the U.S. Army four months later. 2nd Lt. Buckles grave indicated he was a member of the 8th Infantry Regiment, 4th Infantry Division.

Hill 578 – 8th Infantry Regiment – C Company

Personal Account by Chaplain Bruno Luechinger

To most of the 8th Infantry Regiment, Hill 578 is a number on a map but to the men of C Company it represents a period of two weeks which will not soon be forgotten.

When the Company was given the mission of taking the hill, it seemed a long way from where we were although in fact it was only a matter of a thousand yards or so. Between us and the hill were Boku Gerries who effectively allowed us down because of their well dug in positions in the heavy woods. Rather than cross a draw directly to the hill, Lt. Gude decided on a wide end run, moving due North, then Northeast and finally swinging to the Southeast thru a draw and on up to the hill. It was a cautious but steady move and had it not been for an exceptionally thick fog, our presence in the vicinity of the hill would certainly have been detected by the enemy. As it was, we were able to get to the top of the hill and Lt. Gude immediately placed his platoons for a perimeter defense. Violating everything in the Book, the Command Post was placed in a small clump of trees on the very top. This spot later proved to be the safest place on the hill although surrounded on all sides by an open area varying from 60 to 160 yards. The Company was greatly understrength and the defense line was necessarily very thin. However, the men realized the importance of holding the hill and set to work securing and digging in in the best possible spots. The objective was reached at approximately 1400 and immediately I registered in Company C to be prepared for any future enemy action. Getting rolls that night was out of the question. Rations and water were in the same category. A small running stream at the foot of the hill where we approached the hill solved the water problem temporarily. The lack of blankets was not the only factor which lessened sleep that night. Every man was on the alert for trouble of any kind.

September 19 – Because of the need for rations, a combat ration patrol of about 25 men under Sgt. Odis Malone retraced their route of the preceding day back to Battalion. Once there, they were unable to return because of the artillery and cannon fire being placed in the draws between the battalion and the hill. Four men were killed while in the Battalion area from a heavy shelling by rockets. The rest of the patrol arriving back at the hill at dusk bringing the best K rations ever put out. The one supper unit Lt. Gude and I had rationed between us from the preceding morning had been consumed. That morning Lt. Woodruff and Lt. Fremont Burdick took the 1st platoon with one section of light machine guns and one mortar squad back along a road leading to B Company. Shortly after leaving the draw they ran into the enemy dug in thru the woods. A heavy fire fight followed and the platoon drove the enemy out of the woods, killing 7 by actual count and taking 8 prisoners and then returned to the hill. The Field Artillery did not have a forward observer with C Company so I registered it in in the draw between our B Company and the 22nd Infantry Regiment as observation from the top of the hill was excellent in all directions except the Southeast. I also registered in the 81mm mortar. To the east and northeast during the afternoon several groups of Gerries were spotted and Cannon Company fired a number of missions. It was worth the price of admission to see them scatter when the rounds started landing. That night the movement of what we thought were horse drawn carts was heard to the Southeast and a few concentrations of 105's soon stopped that. The enemy was without question bringing in personnel and supplies.

September 20 – Lt. Woodruff took 25 men and forked his way back along the route cleared the day before and established a supply route from B Company to the draw at the foot of the hill. Rations and rolls were brought up. Blankets and shelter halves were never more welcome as the weather was definitely not on the dry or warm side. Just as it was getting dark, a large number of the enemy was observed to the left front heading for the draws surrounding the hill. Earlier in the day artillery and cannon concentrations to the rear, both flanks and to the front had been fired and numbered. With the start of all the enemy activity, I fired both the artillery and Cannon Company simultaneously, the latter on the left and front and the former on the right and rear. The effect was that we completely boxed ourselves in with our own supporting fires. Cannon Company guns were kept hot until shortly after 0200 in the morning. At that time the outposts reported everything quiet so all firing ceased.

September 21 - Cannon Company resumed firing at approximately 0500, covering Hill 569 and the draws on either side of it. About 0530, Gerries were heard and observed in the edge of the woods almost due west and in the rear of the Command Post. An immediate call for artillery was made in the area of the schoolhouse and from there it was walked North and East until a concentration hit near the edge of the woods. I hesitated to bring it in any closer but Lt. Gude who was there with me gave me the OK and after warning all the men to stay in their holes we brought it in the final 100 yards. At that point it was landing not over 90 yards from where we were and 60 yards from the 3rd platoon. The risk in bringing in the artillery so close paid for itself many times over even the shrapnel was practically playing My Country Tis of Thee because it was coming right toward us. That last 100 yards caught them where the hair was short and their screams and hollering were almost as loud as the bursts themselves. Fire in the same place was repeated twice more and each time the screams increased. Both Gude and I got hit by shrapnel but neither of us was hurt at all. Lt. Skinner added the support of the 60 mm mortars during the big shoot and all in all it was not a quiet affair. Lt. Gude and I thru an interpreter gave the survivors a chance to surrender but the offer was refused. About 0930 B Company started its advance thru the woods which had been shelled and all artillery in the area was lifted. During the course of the day Cannon Company fired numerous times as targets of opportunity to the East and Southeast. The 3rd platoon held hill 569 during the day but pulled back that night. Lt. Matyka led a combat patrol in the direction of the schoolhouse but did not have sufficient strength to reach it but the patrol did see the devastating effect of the artillery fire of the morning and as one Frenchman, George, gesticulated, they had to step over German bodies.

About dark that night the 2nd platoon outpost reported the enemy digging in in the open area from the edge of Hill 569 to the draw. Upon listening we could hear them plainly up at the CP. After several concentrations of 105 from Cannon Company they could be heard moving to the Southeast thru the draw between Hills 578 and 569. We shifted the fire right with them and twice there was a repetition of the screaming heard that morning. All night long we could hear them moaning and praying in that area. Fire in the draw to the Southeast was continued almost all night as the sound of troop and cart movements could be heard at the Command Post. Many taxpayers would scream too if they knew the cost of the ammo fired in this one 24-hour period. Nine truckloads of Cannon besides all the field artillery and mortars. My poor aching back!!

September 22 – Lt. Matyka's platoon went to Hill 569 while the rest of the company started an attack Southwest to the schoolhouse. The company met continued resistance but by eliminating one enemy machine gun at a time it was able to keep moving forward. It was held up by a machine gun across a steep draw and Sgt. Lewis with his light machine gun killed the gunner thus permitting the company to advance across the draw. The company made excellent use of its 60mm mortars and they kept firing ahead of the company and the company got to within 75 yards of the objective, the schoolhouse. At this point Lt. Gude was hit by a sniper's bullet in the right shoulder and he was brought back up to the Command Post. Lt. Mache of the medics arrived in about half an hour and dressed the wound and just as the evacuating jeep pulled away with Gude, an enemy machine gun opened up on it. We could not even evacuate the wounded safely. Lt. Woodruff took over and held the ground gained until he withdrew back to the hill as the unit moving forward toward the schoolhouse from the Southwest was unable to move forward and tie in with our company. It was several hours after Gude was hit before Woody got back up on the hill and in the meantime Gerries had infiltrated between hill 569 and 578 thus cutting off Lt. Matykas platoon. I acted as a coordinator between all parties and battalion besides firing a number of missions at the same time. Temporarily acting as a company commander of a rifle company was a little out of my line but I will always be glad that it was C Company, a group of men who cannot be surpassed or even equaled in the United States Army (men serving in Company C included Wayne Johnson, Francisco Delgado, Bill Loy, Odis Malone and the authors relative and Medal of Honor recipient Pedro Cano, all superb and brave soldiers). During that day 20 prisoners were captured, including one Captain. We had several killed and several wounded. Lt. Matyka was able to infiltrate his platoon back from hill 569 without casualties. A few minutes after Lt. Gude was evacuated, several of our men were ambushed at the stream and the jeep carrying chow was fired on. One or two men are still missing and there went our water supply again. After

Matyka got back, I put more fire on 569 and the area to the Southeast and artillery fire was also directed in the area. We heard noise in the draw so continued firing a good part of the night.

September 23 – Lt. Woodruff again led the Company in an attack toward the schoolhouse. This was successfully done and contact with F Company of the 22nd Infantry Regiment was made and a new supply line to and from Battalion was then secured. That night was the first time we had any real rations from Battalion and the same applied to radio batteries and numerous other things which we needed badly. The 2nd platoon was outposted some 200 yards to the front and thus they were able to cut two roads and the road junction between hills 578 and 569. B Company placed an outpost in the draw and to the Northwest and again the water supply was ours. Lt. Skinner shot and killed a Kraut 30 feet from his fox hole. The enemy by this time must surely have known that we had every draw and spot in that whole terrain covered with our artillery concentrations but yet he continued all thru the day and that night to attempt to come in thru the draws and get in our rear. Some groups were able to actually observe and others only hear but they all got artillery shells on them from either Cannon Company or the 29th Field. That night we got some C rations and they were a relief from the K's.

September 24 – Spent most in further improving the defensive position and in patrol to the front and flanks. On patrol captured 2 more prisoners.

September 25 – Further patrols and completion of the defense, including the stringing of barbed wire. This was necessary as the line was so thin that it was impossible otherwise to cover the whole damned perimeter of that hill. Lt. Fremont Burdick and Sgt. Francisco Delgado (who would be awarded DSC for action in Hurtgen Forest on December 2nd and 3rd), a BAR man, while on a private little patrol observed an entire enemy squad coming down a road along the trees on hill 569. They waited until the enemy were within 35 yards and then opened up. Only one survived. Battalion gave the company the mission of securing a prisoner and this was accomplished by a patrol which crawled over 50 yards in the open and under enemy observation and brought back a wounded Gerry who had been injured the night before by our artillery. This man was immediately sent back to Battalion. That night enemy were heard in the draw to the Southeast but a few rounds of 105 soon fixed that situation. There was plenty of artillery fired during the day.

September 26 – Lt. Shearer and his patrol, doing a beautiful job, got within a few feet of a guard on the enemy's right flank. This patrol upon returning accurately pinpointed the enemy position and another patrol from Lt. Matykas platoon located 3 machine guns on hill 569. After all patrols were in Cannon Company shelled both spots and the next morning a patrol reported evacuated positions and at least 6 dead Krauts that they could see.

September 27 – An enemy patrol tried to get through our lines but an alert outpost fired and dispersed it. Sgt. Garrecht on patrol located enemy digging in in the draw immediately to our front. This area got the same treatment as all other suspected enemy spots and the next morning there were not any enemy around. Their only virtue was their persistence. About midnight an outpost reported some noises on Hill 569 so there went more taxpayer's money but Lt. Matyka the following morning found where we had made a direct hit on an enemy mortar and hastily abandoned positions. Evidently the enemy had intended to give us a little mortar fire but we beat him to the draw, thanks to an alert outpost.

September 28 and until we got off the hill some 16 days after we hit it, were spent in daily patrols and ducking the rockets which Gerry threw over every day. Every time that rocket gun opened up, Cannon Company threw rounds out in the general direction and managed to limit it to one burst. Every day there were numerous targets for artillery fire.

The men of C Company did a swell job. One prisoner reported on the 4th day we were on the hill that only 60 out of a whole Battalion survived our artillery. After that we know we got a lot more. We also know that Gerry evacuated a lot of his dead, our GRO took over about 100 bodies and the GRO of the 22nd another large number of them. The accurate placing of artillery would have been impossible had it not been for the constant alertness of the outposts and guards. They aided in the adjustment of the fire when the enemy was too close for the use of the radio any place except on the top of the hill. More than once artillery was brought in within 75 yards of them and they welcomed it.

In spite of the rainy miserably cold weather and constant shelling and harassment from the enemy, the morale of the men remained ace high. That was their hill and it would have taken about 10 enemy divisions to ever divest them of it. This is just a summary of the highlights of Hill 578. It is by no means a complete history of all that happened.[112] This concluded Chaplain Bruno Luechinger's account of Hill 578. After serving as 1st Battalion Chaplain for the entire war, Chaplain Luechinger returned to civilian life in December 1945 and was discharged as a Major from the Officer's Reserve Corps in 1953. He continuously served in five campaigns: Normandy, Northern France, Rhineland, Ardennes, Central Europe. He was awarded the Silver Star Medal, American Campaign Medal, European African Middle Eastern Medal, World War II Victory Medal and Distinguished Unit Badge.

---

[112] Hill 578 8th Infantry Regiment – C Company Personal Account by Chaplain Luechinger

A Chaplain Remembered

Father Julius Sullivan gave the following account, "After his separation from the service in December 1945, Father Bruno was appointed Mission Secretary and Director of the Seraphic Mass Association for the Province, assigned to St. John's. It was the Seraphic Mass Association that occupied him until death. He enlarged the office staff and through business-like improvement of the operation, by building up an army of promoters, he raised enrollments to an all-time level. Father Bruno was at the beck and call of missionaries anytime and anywhere. Requests poured in as varied as a scholarship for a native of Turkey to a sewing machine for a widow in Okinawa. His work not only entailed a massive correspondence, but the know-how of purchasing and expediting and even packing. At the time of his death, he had just finished shipping arrangements for an order of supplies to the Capuchin Missions of Chile which had been devastated in a series of earthquakes. Items included furnaces, cement mixers, plumbing fixtures, a truck and a jeep. The whole order was financed by the General Secretariat and handled in New York. The secret of father Bruno's power must be sought in the motives which animated him. We know from his written and spoken words of his conviction that by helping the missions he could win the blessings of God. And behind the man of action was the man of prayer, holy priest and selfless religious. He was a self-disciplined man. Despite his poor health he appeared with unfailing regularity at morning prayers and 630 saw him on his way to say Mass at Our Lady's altar. There was something appropriate in the way Sister Death came to him, at work in his office. The clatter of typewriters and the jungle of telephones provided the somewhat unmonastic setting for the final summons.

Between the moment that he collapsed and the second he breathed his last, seven precious minutes elapsed, during which, fully conscious, he received the last rites from the hands of his brethren. May the souls of all those he helped, at home, on the battlefield, in the missions, intercede for him before the throne of God."[113]

Father Bruno, is buried in the Capuchin cemetery at Sacred Heart Monastery in Yonkers, New York with his many confreres he shared his life with. There are over 21 Capuchin friars who are American veterans in the cemetery. They even have five Capuchins from England in the cemetery. One being Fr. Cyprian Truss who served for four years in the Royal Flying Corps in France, becoming a flight commander. He was present on April 21, 1918 when Manfred von Richtofen, the famous Red Barron, was shot down over France.[114]

---

[113] Tribute to Father Bruno, Father Julius Sullivan, O.F.M. Cap.

[114] Br. Roger Deguire O.F.M. Cap Letter

Old Officers Return

By the end of September 1944, many of the old officers and men who had been wounded during the first campaign in Normandy and in subsequent engagements during the drive across France, were returned to duty. Six officers, among whom was 2nd Lt. Herbert W. Wittenberger, returned to duty from various replacement pools with seventy-eight experienced enlisted men.[115] Wittenberger, wounded in June during the invasion, was born in Carleton, Nebraska, and had worked at Raymond Bauer Drug Store prior to the war as well as attended the University of Nebraska. He had married Miss Lillian Rose on August 27,1943 in a candle-light ceremony in New York City. In October 1944, Wittenberger would be promoted to Captain and Battalion S-2 Commander. He would survive the war but the toll of war was heavy and he would die about a year after the war ended. His grave indicated he was a Captain and member of 1st BN HDQ CO, 8th INF REG, 4th DIV. As the old officers and enlisted men returned, the casualty lists increased in length. The 8th Infantry Regiment, having constantly spearhead successive drives from the Normandy Beachhead into the Siegfried defenses was battle-worn and weary. Men who remained at the front unwounded throughout the many engagements which had been fought since the 6th of June, asked themselves and each other, "Will it ever end?"[116]

---

[115] 8th Regiment Daily Summaries
[116] 8th Regiment Daily Summaries

Captain Crisson Escapes Capture

Closer engagements would follow and lead to Captain Crisson being captured by a German patrol in early October 1944. Captain Crisson, "I had checked "I" and "L" Companies CP's and passed down a fire lane on my way to "K" Company to check their positions. I met two soldiers from "K" Company who pointed out to me one of their mortar positions in a nearby thicket. I was traveling alone, and when entered the thicket, two Germans were waiting with their rifles cocked. These two Germans did not have dug-in positions in that immediate area. I believe they had either been on patrol and moved in the night before through a gap between the 8th's and 12th's contact companies, or else, they had been bypassed in our attack and were operating behind the lines. One was 18 or 20 years old. The other was about 30. Both were privates wearing German uniforms, wearing overcoats as their outer garments. They spoke English fluently."[117]

Captain Crisson continued, "I started on my inspection about 1800, so I estimate my capture to have been about 1830. My pistol was removed and my pockets searched for military information. All I had, were a few personal letters from which our unit identification was learned. All papers were left on my person. They ordered me to go with them, and we started walking toward the West. We walked toward our mortar position for I could hear them firing. We changed direction and walked toward the South. I had the impression that they knew what they were doing and where they were going. One of our mortar barrages landed where we were walking. This frightened and confused the Germans. None of us were injured, though

---

[117] Capt. Robert Crisson Statement, October 19, 1944

68

a piece of shrapnel tore my coat and pant leg. The Germans decided to get some information from me, although, I was of the opinion that they were trying to take me to their headquarters. From my letters they learned that I was an officer, however, when I refused to answer their questions I was beaten. Their questions were about the disposition of our troops and heavy weapons. I did not answer their questions and was hit in the face, knocked to the ground and kicked in the stomach. I pretended to be dead, but changed my mind when they decided to shoot me to make sure I was dead. I got to my feet, and we started off again. I was in a dazed condition, but I thought we were walking toward the East. Their actions still impressed me as if they knew where they were going. Suddenly, small arms fire (friendly) opened up to our rear. The bullets were not aimed at us, for I didn't hear them whiz past. This action confused and completely unsettled the Germans. They ran for cover, and in their excitement, forgot about me. I took advantage of this scramble by turning and running in the opposite direction from which they were taking me. I ran through the underbrush until I passed out from exhaustion."[118]

Captain Crisson, "I had lost all sense of time and cannot say how long I was unconscious, I continued traveling in the same direction. Again, I passed out from exhaustion. This time I regained consciousness just before dark and could hear Americans talking near me. I walked in their direction and called to them. I came out on a road. I hailed a passing jeep and asked the occupants to take me to an aid station. I was received at the 2nd Battalion, 12th Infantry's aid station at 1900 and given medical treatment by Capt. Ware."[119] Due to being seriously wounded, Captain Crisson was evacuated through medical channels at 0800 but would return in early October.

---

[118] Capt. Robert Crisson Statement, October 19, 1944

[119] Capt. Robert Crisson Statement, October 19, 1944

Captain Crisson Returns to Battalion

He worked at headquarters for the next few months but had an interesting story on the matter in a letter to his mother dated March 7, 1945, "I am sure feeling good. I have all of my weight back and there is absolutely nothing wrong with me. I am also very happy, too. My old Regimental Commander asked for me to come back to the 8th Infantry. The old man said that it was entirely up to me and that if I wanted to return, he would not hold me back, because he said that he could easily understand how I felt about it. Well, I am back with the good old 8th Infantry, the best fighting Regiment in the world. I am with the Second Battalion. I have many of my old boys over here too. It is just like old times. Mother, please don't be angry with me. I got pretty mad at one of my friends up at the HQ the other day when I told him that I was going back to the line. He said, "Cris, don't do that. Don't be a fool!" I just looked at him sitting there on his broad buttock and I felt absolutely sick way down deep inside. I even felt somewhat ashamed for not having protested more when the old man pulled me out of the line before. I hated to think that I had been working so far to the rear for these past 2 or 3 months. I could only look at him and shake my head. I was thinking about some of the things my boys had been through and then seeing him sitting there, never having been in the line. Doing a job that was necessary, but one that some combat officer should be transferred to in order to get a rest, and I got even sicker. There he was and he had said, "Cris, don't be a fool." Before I turned away I just held my temper and said, "Well,_____, I know several thousand pals who have been fighting for a long time. That's why we're sitting in Germany now." Oh mother, you don't need to worry about me. I have learned so very much about combat. And my experience in Division Headquarters has helped me in such a way that now together with that experience and my actual combat experience, I feel capable of commanding a Battalion. Oh, I have commanded a battalion for short periods, but I always felt that I should learn much more, because too many lives were at stake. Right now, I am second in command of the 2nd Battalion and as soon as a vacancy comes in, they are going to give me a battalion."[120]

---

[120] Capt. Robert Crisson Letter, March 7, 1945, Megan Snow

Anniversary of D-Day – Captain Crisson

In April 1945, Capt. Crisson was promoted to Major upon his return to the First Battalion.

On the anniversary of D-Day in 1945, he addressed his men.

June 5, 1945 Major Crisson, Battalion Commander,
To The Officers And Men Of The First Battalion
Our Battalion, The First Battalion, has established one of the finest combat records of this war. Of the two battalions selected from the entire United States First Army for the assault on the German West Wall (Utah Beach) in Normandy, ours was one. Because of this selection, you can see that our fine reputation did not begin with the initial landing in Normandy. It began many years ago. Our training results had always been superior. Not only that, but all of our companies are well represented throughout the entire Army. General George C. Marshall was once a member of our Battalion. Maj. General Raymond O. Barton, our former Division Commander, commanded the First Battalion during World War One. Brig. General Muller, Third Army G-4, commanded two of our companies at various times during World War One. The First Battalion has produced numerous other generals who are in the Army today.

There is not enough space in this paper for me to relate more than a fraction of the "impossible" missions accomplished by our Battalion during the European War. It isn't even necessary because you were there making it possible for them to be accomplished. You know! You did it!

You have each and every one done a splendid job in combat. Not only that, but you have reverted from the role of a combat soldier to that of a garrison soldier and I would like to compare you with any garrison unit anywhere. A good soldier is good no matter what kind of life he is living… combat or garrison…he will always look good.

We are not letting General Marshall down. He could see us at any time and be proud to say, "That is my old outfit!"[121]

---

[121] First Battalion, 8th Regiment Newsletter, June 5, 1945

A Rediscovered Note

On that fateful day on June 5, 1944, Captain Robert C. Crisson sought out 27 men to sign a French Note and began a story that would represent virtually every American land and sea element attacking Utah Beach on D-day. And now almost 77 years later, that story has been rediscovered and expanded. Each brave soldier had his own hope, faith and fears in surviving the battle before them. Many would never see each other again. Some died on the battlefield and some were seriously wounded but all fought courageously. By their combined effort, these incredible men began the fight to save the world from a madman. May their stories inspire future generations to seek out the unknown and forgotten stories of the greatest generation in American history.

The Note Men

Lt. Col. Conrad Christopher Simmons
Albany, New York
1st Battalion Commander
Silver Star / Purple Heart
Killed in Action - June 24, 1944

Lt. Col. Conrad Simmons lived in NYC his whole life and eventually applied for officers training as WWI was ending. He was commissioned as an officer in late 1918 and served in the Army as a Second Lieutenant until being discharged in 1919. Knowing the war was over, but still wanting to be a part of the military, Conrad enlisted in the New York National Guard in 1919 with the 51st New York Machine Gun Squadron. During this time back in New York, he studied at Columbia University, earning a Bachelors of Science and starting up a road construction company. Eventually, the machine gun squadron was converted into the 101st New York Anti Tank Battalion, and Conrad was named its commander. The 101st was federalized in 1941 and attached to the 8th Infantry Regiment, which was sent overseas. Conrad and the 8th participated in the D-Day landing. Conrad was killed on June 24, 1944. He is buried in the Normandy American Cemetery of Colleville.

**Major John Henry Meyer
Gainesville, Florida
Executive Officer - 1st
Battalion
Silver Star
Died 12-03-2001**

John Henry Meyer, was a decorated WWII battalion commander. Meyer was born in New Orleans on November 2, 1914 and grew up in his family home, "Promised Land" in Plaquemines Parish, LA. He attended the US Military Academy at West Point, NY and graduated in the class of 1939. He married Miss Mary Alice Hampton. He was the 1st Battalion Executive Officer of the 8th Infantry Regiment during the 4th Division's assault at Utah Beach in June 1944. He led his battalion across France through Luxemburg and Germany in five campaigns. After the war, he attended the Command and General Staff College and the National War College. He served as Tactical Officer at West Point, on the Army Staff in War Plans Division, and on the staff of the National Security Council. In Germany during the Cold War years, he served as a Battle Group and Brigade Commander, and then, as Chief of Staff of the 3rd Infantry Division. After earning a Master's Degree at George Washington university in International Affairs, he joined the Faculty of the National War College before he retired in 1968. Col. Meyer's military decorations include the Combat Infantryman's Badge, two Presidential Union Citations, the Silver Star Medal, three Bronze Star medals, two Purple Hearts, the Legions of Merit, the Luxembourg Croix de Guerre and the Belgian Fourragere. He retired an Army Colonel. Colonel Meyer died on December 3, 2001 at his home in Charlottesville, VA.

Captain George Gregory Holochwost
Philadelphia, Penn
29ᵗʰ Field Artillery (8ᵗʰ Infantry Regiment)
Wounded in Action – June 6, 1944
Silver Star
Died 6-13-1976

GEORGE G. HOLOCHWOST
Major
Battalion S-3
5703 Forest Rd.
Cheverly, Md.

George G. Holochost was born on May 3, 1914 in Brooklyn, New York. He received his BS at Cornell University, Class of 1937. His occupation was a fruit and vegetable inspector. He married Magda Gabriella Cariaggi in 1940. During his stay in the U.S. Army, he was awarded he Silver Star, Bronze Star and Purple Heart. He retired from the U.S. Army in June 1967, rising to the rank of Major. In 1964 George joined The Corps of Cadets at Texas A&M University commanding Company G. George passed away on June 11, 1976. He was buried in Barrington, Rhode Island.

1st Lt. Charles Harmon Jones DSC
Antigo, Wisconsin
1st Battalion Headquarter (Staff Intelligence Officer)
Distinguished Service Cross / Purple Heart
Killed in Action - June 10, 1944

1ˢᵗ Lt. Charles Harmon Jones was born on March 23, 1918 in Bryant, Wisconsin. He graduated from high school and was a stenographer and typist at the People's Bank in Antigo. On June 10, 1944, Charlie was killed in Normandy

as part of the D-Day invasion. He was awarded the Distinguished Service Cross for his actions and bravery. He is buried in Bryant, Wisconsin.

2nd Lt. Herbert Walker Wittenberger
Carleton, Nebraska
1st Battalion Staff
Wounded in Action – June 1944
Became S-2 10/44
Died 6-20-1947

Herbert Walker Wittenberger was born on August 18, 1918 in Carleton, Nebraska. He worked at Raymond Bauer Drug Store. Herbert attended the University of Nebraska. He married Miss Lillian Rose on August 27, 1943 in a candle-light ceremony in New York City. They made their home in Trenton, New Jersey.

HERBERT W. WITTENBERGER
First Lieutenant
S-2
Carleton, Nebr.

On D-Day June 6, 1944 he landed on Utah Beach as a 2nd Lt. with head-quarters, 1st Battalion, 8th Infantry Regiment. Herbert was wounded in June 1944 during the Normandy invasion. In October 1944, he rose to become the battalion S-2. He rose to the rank of Captain. Herbert survived the war but died on June 27, 1947 at age 28. He is buried in Carleton, Nebraska. His grave indicates he was a Captain and member of 1st BN HDQ CO, 8th INF REG, 4th DIV.

Captain John Richard Garrabrant
Wilmington, North Carolina
1st Battalion Headquarter Staff
Distinguished Service Cross / Purple Heart
Kill in Action – June 10, 1944

John Richard Garrabrant was born in East Orange, New Jersey on May 23, 1916. By 1930 he and his family had moved to New Hanover High School, North Carolina. He attended North Carolina State University where for four years he was a member of the R.O.T.C. On July 20, 1940, he married Emily Reckling and in 1941 they had a son. After graduating

college Garrabrant worked for the Atlantic Coast Line Railroad in North Carolina. In 1941 he entered active duty in the Army. He trained for four more years at various U.S. Army bases. He arrived in England in January 1944 with the rest of the 4th Infantry Division to begin D-Day preparations. On D-Day June 6, 1944 he landed on Utah Beach as a captain with head-quarters, 1st Battalion, 8th Infantry Regiment. The Commanding Officer of Company C, 8th Infantry, Captain Robert C. Crisson was wounded on the day of the landing and Garrabrant was directed to take command of the Company. On June 10, 1944, Garrabrant was killed during an advance of his battalion near Montebourg. His act of valor during that engagement earned him the Distinguished Service Cross. Garrabrant was buried in the temporary American Military Cemetery at Ste. Mere Eglise. By mid-July his family had not yet been notified of his death but his wife Emily knew, as she had heard from a friend whose husband had served with Garrabrant and wrote of his death. Emily kept that news from the family and harbored the hope it was wrong and that he might still be alive. However, she soon received the dreaded telegram informing her of his death. On December 15, 1944 his Distinguished Service Cross was presented to Emily at the First Presbyterian Church in Wilmington, North Carolina, by the Commanding General of Fort Bragg. After the war Garrabrant's remains reinterred and he was laid to his final rest in Plot E Row 17 Grave 8, Normandy American Cemetery at Colleville-sur-Mer, Normandy, France.

Lt. Chester Leroy Palmer
Houston, TX
USNR (United States Naval Reserve)
Seriously Wounded in Action –
June 8, 1944
Died 12-16-1997

Lt. Chester Leroy Palmer was born in Drumright, Oklahoma on April 29, 1920. He grew up in Houston, Texas where he attended Rice University and worked at Humble Oil & Refinery as a Boiler-Maker helper. He enlisted in the U.S. Navy on August 10, 1942. He served on the U.S.S.

Nevada. On D-Day June 6, 1944 he landed on Utah Beach with the 1st Battalion, 8th Infantry Regiment. Leroy was spotting gunfire from the Battleship Nevada. He was in a tree when he was shot by a sniper. He received a Purple Heart. He would eventually return home and marry Miss Jean Gillie. He would earn his doctorate degree. Dr. Palmer retired in 1990 from a teaching career that spanned forty-five years, the last 25 years at Buffalo State College. Dr. Palmer died on December 17, 1997. He was buried in Tonawanda, New York.

1st Lt. Gail Bruce Lee
Tallahassee, Florida
Commander B Company
Distinguished Service Cross/Bronze Star/Purple Heart
Wounded in Action – June 10, 1944
Died 2-21-1970

Gail Bruce Lee was born in Mississippi on February 22, 1916. However, the 1920 Census indicates Gail was born in Louisiana. His mother, Evilina, was also born in Louisiana. Gail was 1 of 13 children. He was a farm hand and worked on general farms. He enlisted in the National Guard on November 25, 1940. He was raised in Walthall, Mississippi and completed at least three years of high school. On D-Day June 6, 1944 he landed on Utah Beach with the 1st Battalion, 8th Infantry Regiment. He was the Commander of B Company. Lee was wounded on June 10, 1944. He was awarded the Distinguished Service Cross for his actions on that day. He would also be awarded the Bronze Star, Purple Heart, Combat Infantryman badge, and the Presidential Unit Citation. Lee had a war time wedding with an all military twist in Pensacola, Florida on May 4, 1945. He married 2nd Lt. Enid E. Erwin, ANC, lately returned from duty in the United Kingdom, and assigned to duty at Welch Convalescent hospital in Daytona Beach. The Maid of Honor was Cpl. Margaret Erwin, WAC, sister of the bride and the bride's brother, Maj. Wallace Erwin, was best man. Lt. Erwin joined the Army Nurse Corps in August 1942. She served in England, Ireland, and Scotland from September 1943, until December 1944. She had her share of robot bombs and the hospital where she was stationed in England, cared for men wounded in the invasion. Paratroopers were on their operating tables even before the infantry landed, as they were flown back to England.

Captain Lee was wounded four days after landing on Utah Beach. He was evacuated to the hospital in which Lt. Erwin was serving, and it was there, that they met. Lt. Erwin and Captain Lee met in the hospital in England, they were evacuated on the same hospital ship to the United States, sent to the same general hospital, and after a brief honeymoon, both returned to Welch Convalescent hospital, where Captain Lee was also assigned. Captain Lee would stay in the U.S. Army after the war and fight in the Korean War where he became a Lt. Colonel. His service ended in Pensacola, Florida.

2nd Lt. William Dayton Baucum
Springhill, Louisiana
C Company – Boat 7
Seriously Wounded in Action – June 10,1944
Died 9-07-1985

William Dayton Baucum was born on March 24, 1913 in Springhill, Louisiana. He worked for Webster Parish School Board. He enlisted in the U.S. Army on April 21, 1943. On D-Day June 6, 1944 he landed on Utah Beach with the 1st Battalion, 8th Infantry Regiment as a member of C Company. He was seriously wounded on June 10, 1944. He departed the U.S. Army on January 1, 1946. William married Iris Taylor. He was a life long resident of Springhill. He was an active member of the Springhill United Methodist Church, member of the Administrative Board, Lay leader and teacher of Men's Bible Class, He retired from the Webster Parish School System with 34 years of service, where he served as a teacher, coach, principal and Parish supervisor. William died on September 7, 1985 and is buried in Springhill, Louisiana.

2nd Lt. Edward Henry Buckles
Long Beach, California
Purple Heart
Killed in Action – September 20, 1944

1st Lt. Edward Henry Buckles was born on October 1, 1920 in Kansas City, Missouri. He moved to Long Beach, California. He worked nearby at the U.S. Navy on Terminal Island in San Pedro as a cost inspector of Bethlehem Steel. Edwards married Patricia C Parmenter on May 19, 1942. Edward enlisted in the U.S. Army on September 11, 1942. On D-Day June 6, 1944 he landed on Utah Beach with the 1st Battalion, 8th Infantry Regiment. Lt. Buckles was killed in battle on September 20, 1944. Lt. Buckles was buried in Long Beach, California. His grave indicated he was a member of the 8th Infantry Regiment, 4th Infantry Division.

2nd Lt. Fremont Ralph Burdick
Oak Valley, Rhode Island
C Company – Boat 9
Seriously Wounded in Action – June 9, 1944
Bronze Star
Died 8-09-1977

FREMONT R. BURDICK
First Lieutenant
Assistant Special Services
Officer
Hope Valley, R. I.

2nd Lt. Fremont Ralph Burdick was born on March 3, 1920 in Hope Valley, Rhode Island. He was a student at Rhode Island State Colle in Kingston, Rhode Island. On D-Day June 6, 1944 he landed on Utah Beach with the 1st Battalion, 8th Infantry Regiment as a member of C Company. He was seriously wounded on June 9, 1944. He earned a Bronze Star. He would stay in the U.S. Army after the war was over and rise to the rank of Lt. Colonel and fight in the Korean War and Vietnam War. Burdick died on August 9, 1977. He is buried in Hopkinton, Rhode Island .

Kenneth Gale Crawford
War Correspondent
First newsman to wade ashore on Normandy on D-Day
Died 1-14-1983

Kenneth Gale Crawford was born on May 27, 1902 in Sparta, Wisconsin. As a Washington correspondent he was a confidant of presidents from

Roosevelt to Nixon. As a war correspondent, he was the first newsman to wade ashore in Normandy on D-Day in 1944. On D-Day June 6, 1944 he landed on Utah Beach with the 1st Battalion, 8th Infantry Regiment with members of C Company led by Captain Robert Crisson. Crawford went to work for the United Press in Chicago in 1924 after graduating from Beloit College in Wisconsin. After working in the United Press Milwaukee, St. Paul, Detroit and St.  Louis bureaus he came to Washington for the United Press in 1927 and was immediately assigned to cover the White House. Crawford became a Newsweek columnist and reported for them during the D-Day invasion. During World War II he reported from North Africa, Egypt, Turkey, Italy, England and France. Crawford registered for the WWII draft on February 16, 1942. 'Ken Crawford set a shining example for a couple of generations of journalists in this town,' said Washington Post executive Editor Benjamin Bradlee, who worked under Crawford in Newsweek's Washington Bureau in the 1950's. 'Through his dedication to lean, explicit prose and to the fairness and integrity he set high standards for all of us.' Crawford and Captain Robert Crisson stayed in contact for many years after the war. Crawford was in Crisson's boat that came ashore on Utah Beach on D-Day. Crawford married Elizabeth Bartholomew on July 16, 1928 and remained married to her his entire life. Crawford died on January 13, 1983. He was buried in Harbor Beach, Michigan.

Capt. Albert Matthews Krekler
Clinton, Indiana
6th Armored Group
70th Tank Battalion
Wounded in Action five times (6-44,
7-15-44, 8-7-44, 9-29-44)
Silver Star, Bronze Star, Purple Heart
(5 Clusters)
Died 1-31-1981

Captain Albert Matthews Krekler was born on December 15, 1911 in West Elkton, Ohio. He was a graduate of Indiana University. He moved to Clinton, Indiana. He worked at A & P Tea Company in Greencastle, Indiana. On D-Day June 6, 1944 he landed on Utah Beach with the 1st Battalion, 8th Infan-

Major Albert Matthews Lundy Krekler
in Europe, WWII

try Regiment. Krekler would be wounded five times and be awarded the Silver Star, Bronze Star and Purple heart (5 clusters). On October 20, 1951, Major Krekler was seriously wounded in action by a missile in the North Korea sector. He returned to Indiana to teach English in Hamilton Heights Junior High School. He never married. Krekler died on January 31, 1981 in Indianapolis, Indiana. He is buried in Cicero, Indiana.

Capt. Lucien Martin Strawn
Medical Corps.
Morgantown, West Virginia
Battalion Surgeon
Silver Star
Died 11-12-1988

Dr. Lucien Martin Strawn was born on April 15, 1914 in Uniontown, Pennsylvania. His parents moved to Morgantown, West Virginia where his father was the manager of Canyon Coal and Coke company. Strawn attended col-

LUCIEN M. STRAWN
Captain
Battalion Surgeon
Morgantown, W. Va.

lege at West Virginia University. He married Miss Joy Makinson in 1937. They moved to Pittsburg, Pennsylvania where Strawn worked at the Pittsburg Medical Center. Strawn registered for the draft on October 16, 1940. On D-Day June 6, 1944 he landed on Utah Beach with the 1st Battalion, 8th Infantry Regiment, as the Battalion Surgeon. He earned the Silver Star for bravery in action against the enemy in France. Dr. Strawn passed away on November 12, 1988 in Cumberland, North Carolina. He is buried in Morgantown, West Virginia.

Major Hutson "Hooty" Miller Betty
St. Louis, Missouri
Special Staff – Special Service Officer - Field
Artillery
Died 4-08-1991

HUSTON M. BETTY
Major
Special Service Officer
419 Argonne Dr.
Kirkwood, Mo.

Major Hutson Miller Betty was born on November 17, 1915 in St. Louis, Missouri. He attended Kirkwood High School in Kirkwood, Missouri where he met his future bride, Miss Marian Beecher. They were married on December 13, 1935. Miller attended the University of Missouri where he was the starting center on the football team. He attended the Engineering School. He enlisted in the U.S. Army on February 1, 1941. On D-Day June 6, 1944 he landed on Utah Beach with the 1st Battalion, 8th Infantry Regiment. After the war, Miller and his wife moved to Dewey, Arizona where he was a teacher. Miller passed away on April 8, 1991 in Dewey, Arizona.

Capt. Alfred Francis Birra
Rahway, New Jersey
C.E.(Combat Engineer)
Company C 237th Engineer Combat Battalion
Died 6-20-1984

Captain Alfred Francis Birra was born on October 9, 1914 in Brooklyn, New York. He had two years of college education and worked a variety of jobs to support himself including being a chauffeur driver, bus driver, taxi driver, truck driver and tractor driver. He enlisted in the U.S. Army on February 12, 1942. He married Miss Barbara Ritter on February 24, 1943. Barbara was from Rahway, New Jersey where the couple would soon relocate. On D-Day June 6, 1944 he landed on Utah Beach with the 1st Battalion, 8th Infantry Regiment. Birra would make a career in the U.S. Army and retire as a Lt. Colonel. He passed away on June 20, 1984 in Rahway, New Jersey. He is buried in Arlington National Cemetery.

2nd Lt. Ray William Sherman
Pontiac, Michigan
Wounded in Action – June 15, 1944
Purple Heart
Killed in Action – June 24, 1944

1st Lt. Ray William Sherman was born on March 26, 1918 in Detroit, Michigan. He worked at Grand Trunk-Western Ry in Pontiac, Michigan. He registered for the draft on October 16, 1940. On D-Day June 6, 1944 he landed on Utah Beach with the 1st Battalion, 8th Infantry Regiment. Lt. Sherman was killed on June 24, 1944 and was returned with the WWII Dead program from Carentan, France. Lt. Sherman is buried in Arlington National Cemetery. His grave indicates he was a member of the 8th Infantry Regiment, 4th Infantry Division.

Captain Bruno Luechinger
New York City, New York
1st Battalion Chaplain
Silver Star June 9, 1944
Died 7-20-1961

Captain Bruno Luechinger was born on September 25, 1909 in New York City, New York. He was the son of immigrants. His parents were born in Switzerland

and Austria respectively. He was a student at the St. Anthony's Monastery in Marathon, Wisconsin. He was a teacher at the Monastery of Mary Immaculate and had 5 years or more of college. He became an Ordained Minister at the Catholic Archdiocese of New York. The Rev. Luechinger registered for the draft on October 16, 1940. On D-Day June 6, 1944 he landed on Utah Beach with the 1st Battalion, 8th Infantry Regiment as the 1st Battalion Chaplain. He would serve the entire war as the 1st Battalion Chaplain. He was released from active duty on February 9, 1946. Upon returning home after the war, Rev. Luechinger became the Director of Missions for the Capuchin Province of St.

BRUNO LUECHINGER
Captain
Chaplain
210 W. 31st St.
New York, N. Y.

Mary. On July 20, 1961, Rev. Luechinger died in his office in the rectory of St. John's Church. He was only 52 years old.

2nd Lt. Joseph Phillip Kirby
Minneapolis, Minnesota
C Company - Boat 10
Lightly Wounded in Action – June 8, 1944
Died 10-31-1963

2nd Lt Joseph Phillip Kirby was born on September 30, 1912 in Silver lake, Minnesota. He worked for Jersey Ice Cream Company in Minneapolis, Minnesota. He married Miss Doris Sieckert on March 6, 1933 in Hennepin, Minnesota. On D-Day June 6, 1944 he landed on Utah Beach with the 1st Battalion, 8th Infantry Regiment as a member of C Company. He was lightly wounded in action on June 8, 1944. His U.S. Army service ended on October 28, 1945. 2nd Lt. Kirby passed away on October 31, 1963. He is buried in Ft. Snelling National Cemetery in South Minneapolis, Minnesota.

Captain Ralph Lester Thomas
Beauford, North Carolina
1st Battalion Staff
Silver Star/Bronze Star/Purple Heart
Died 12-20-2008

RALPH L. THOMAS
Major
Executive Officer
Turner St.
Beaufort, N. C.

Captain Ralph Lester Thomas was born on January 19, 1916 in Beaufort, North Carolina. He graduated from Oak Ridge Military Institute and attended the University of Tennessee. He enlisted in the U.S. Army in 1940. On D-Day June 6, 1944 he landed on Utah Beach with the 1st Battalion, 8th Infantry Regiment, as a member of the 1st Battalion Staff. He earned the Silver Star, Bronze Star and Purple Heart and the rank of major in combat through France and Germany. Upon returning home in 1945, he became the country's first Veterans Service Officer. He married Miss Louise Guthrie on July 6 1946. He served as county sheriff from 1966 until 1986. Major Thomas died on December 20, 2008. He is buried in Beaufort, North Carolina.

1st Lt Robert Elwood Ertmer
Freeport, Illinois
1st Battalion
Evacuated from Exhaustion – June 1944
Died 10-19-1980

1st Lt. Robert Elwood Ertmer was born on April 28, 1916 in Mitchell, South Dakota. His family moved to Illinois. He graduated from Aguin High School. Before entering the service, Ertmer was the manager at Krogull Junior Market in Stephenson, Illinois. He enlisted in the U.S. Army on March 5, 1941. He married Miss Alice Mary LaGrand on September 15, 1942 in the Eight Infantry Chapel at Camp Gordon, August, Georgia. The Eighth Infantry Regimental flag and the American flag also stood at the altar. The bride entered the chapel on the arm of Col. John Van Fleet.

Officers of the Eighth Infantry and their wives attended the ceremony. At the time, Ertmer was stationed with Company B, First Battalion, Eighth Infantry at Camp Gordon, Augusta, Georgia. Ertmer was evacuated from France in June or perhaps later of 1944 due to exhaustion. It is not known where he served afterward but his release date was December 11, 1945. 1st Lt. Ertmer passed away on October 19, 1980. He was buried in Wheat Ridge, Colorado. His grave indicated he was a 1st Lt., 4th Infantry Division.

1st Lt. Gerald Showers Doubler
Warren, Illinois
Evacuated due to Exhaustion - June 15, 1944
Died 2-08-1989

1st Lt. Gerald Showers Doubler was born on December 23, 1915 in Warren, Illinois. Doubler graduated from Warren High School and was associated with his father and brothers in farming. For several years he had been a dealer for the DeKalb Agricultural Association until he volunteered for service in the army. He married Beatrye M. Harris on August 8, 1942 in St Charles, Missouri. On D-Day June 6, 1944 he landed on Utah Beach with the 1st Battalion, 8th Infantry Regiment. Ertmer was evacuated due to exhaustion on June 15, 1944. It is not known if he returned to duty but his service release date was September 21, 1944. His never spoke of the war later according to family. The horrors of war were undoubtedly a lifelong burden for so many soldiers. 1st Lt. Doubler passed away on February 8, 1989. He is buried in Warren, Illinois.

1st Lt. Joseph Edwards Samson
Baton Rouge, Louisiana
Commander D Company
Wounded in Action – June 22, 1944
Died 12-28-1972

1st Lt. Joseph Edwards Samson was born on January 9, 1918. He graduated from Louisiana State University. He enlisted in the U.S. Army on February 1, 1942. On D-Day June 6, 1944 he landed on Utah Beach with the 1st Battalion, 8th Infantry Regiment. He was wounded in action on June 22, 1944. He received the Purple Heart. He was released from service on November 23, 1946. 1st Lt. Samson died on December 28, 1972. He was buried in Baton Rouge, Louisiana.

2nd Lt. Richard Eugene Cardoze
Falmouth, Massachusetts
Silver Star – June 10, 1944
Died 11-04-1992

2nd Lt. Richard Eugene Cardoze was born on September 17, 1917 in Falmouth, Massachusetts. He enlisted in the U.S. Army on February 2, 1942. Prior to the war he had at least 2 years of college and worked as an accountant and auditor. On D-Day June 6, 1944 he landed on Utah Beach with the 1st Battalion, 8th Infantry Regiment. For his actions on June 10, 1944, Cardoze was awarded the Silver Star. He was released from service on August 18, 1946. After the war, he returned to Barnstable, Massachusetts. 2nd Lt. Cardoze died on November 4, 1992. He is buried in Arlington National Cemetery.

Lt. Edgar Lawrence Gill
Natchez, Mississippi
U.S.S. Dickman
Died 12-10-1981
USCG

Lt. Edgar Lawrence Gill was born on February 20, 1904 in New Orleans, Louisiana. Prior to the war, he worked at the U.S. Engineer Office. He married Miss Anne Persell on June 27, 1938. He enlisted in the U.S. Coast Guard in 1940 and served on the Joseph T. Dickman on D-Day June 6, 1944, where they transported the 8th Infantry Regiment, 1st Battalion to Utah Beach. Gill rose to the rank of Lt. Commander in WWII. Lt. Gill passed away on December 10, 1981. He is buried in Natchez, Mississippi. His grave indicated he was a Lt. Commander USCG WWII.

Lt. Fendall Perry Williams
Richmond, Virginia
U.S.S. Dickman
USCCR
Died 4-04-1991

Lt. Fendall Perry Williams was born on October 19, 1909 in Richmond, Virginia. After living in Clifton Forge, Virginia, Williams enrolled in the Virginia Military Institute and matriculated in 1928. He was a member of the Class of 1932, the year he graduated, and received a B.A. degree in Liberal Arts. He was a member of the U.S. Army Reserve from 1932 to 1934, the U.S. Marine Corps Reserve from 1935 to 1940, and was a Lieutenant in the U.S. Coast Guard from 1941 to 1964. He eventually rose to the rank of Captain. Williams served on the Joseph T. Dickman on D-Day June 6, 1944, where they transported the 8th Infantry Regiment, 1st Battalion to Utah Beach. He participated in five "D" Landings including Sicily, Salerno, Utah Beach, Southern France and Okinawa. He also Williams married Miss Flo Hope Norris on October 7, 1942. Upon the outbreak of the Korean War, he requested a recall to active service and was ordered to active duty in August 1950. He retired from the Coast Guard in 1964 after having served as chief of Reserve for the Coast Guard in the Twelfth, Thirteenth and Seventeenth Districts. Captain Williams died on April 4, 1991.

French note originally owned by Capt. Robert Crisson, Commander C Company on D Day.

Capt. Robert Carl Crisson
Birmingham, Alabama
Commander C Company
Slightly Wounded in Action – June 6 ,
1944, July 1944, October 1944
Silver Star (June 6, 1944)
Distinguished Service Cross –
July 30, 1944
Purple Heart (three Clusters)
Died 11-16-2013

Capt. Robert Carl Crisson had a distin-
guished career as an officer in the U.S Army spanning 30 years. Crisson joined the Alabama National Guard at age 17 and was later assigned to the Army's 4th Infantry Division, where he worked his way up the ranks to become a commissioned officer. As a 23-year-old company commander, Crisson led the first wave onto Utah Beach on D-Day. Despite being wounded in the assault, Crisson was able to lead his company to secure their objective and advance. He fought in the St. Lo breakthrough, then led his company through the Hedgerows and across Europe, where they fought in the Battle of the Bulge. By the end of the war, Crisson had been promoted

to Major and was the youngest battalion commander in the Army. After the war, he married Miss Ida May Stevens. Crisson served as military advisor during the Greek Civil War in 1950-51 under Gen. James Van Fleet and was the top military advisor to the Chinese Nationalist Forces on Quemoy and Matsu in 1960-61. He was generally regarded throughout his career as the top battlefield commander in the Army, leading the 187th Battle Group of the 82nd Airborne Division from 1962-64. He concluded his military career in 1968 as the Commander of the John F. Kennedy Special Warfare Center, where he led the Green Berets. In Vietnam he later served the U.S. State Department as senior advisor to the ARVN (Vietnamese Army), and as a liaison to the Vietnamese Peace Accords in Saigon in 1973. Crisson's military decorations include the Distinguished Service Cross, two Silver Stars (for valor), three Bronze Stars (for valor), two Legions of Merit, the French Croix de Guerre, and three Purple Hearts. At different times in his career he worked with such luminaries as Ernest Hemingway, Chiang Kai-shek and Madame Chiang, and Robert Kennedy. Col. Robert Crisson passed away peacefully at his home on November 16, 2013 at the age of 92.

Conrad E. Heineman, U.S.J., Albany, N.Y.

John H. Meyer, Major, Louisville, Ky.

George B. Holcomb, Capt. - Phila., Pa.

Garlert Jones, 1st Lt. - Indigo, Miss.

Herbert Watterberg, E.J.A.y. Carlow, Nebr.

John R. Garrabrant, Capt. Wilmington, N.C.

Chester L. Palmer, Lt.(jg) U.S.N.R. Houston, Texas

Fair B. Lee, 400 Waller St., Tallahassee, Fla.

William D. Hansen, 2nd Lt., Gilmer, Texas SPRINGHILL, LA.

Edward H. Buckles, 2nd Lt., L.A. Calif.

Kenneth B. Smith, U.S. Naval, Wis.

R. L. Crawford, San Fran

A. L. ..... Capt. Christine ....

Lewis M. ..... Capt. N.C. Morgantown, W.V.

Hooty Reilly, Maj. F.A. St. Louis, Mo.

Alfred Henn Capt. C.C. Raleigh, New Jersey

R. J. W. Hanmer, 1st Lt. Pontiac, Mich. 14 LINCOLN St.

Bruno Luechinger, Chaplain, 200 West 111 St. New York City

Philip L. Lewis, Col. Lt. Beaufort, N.C.

Robert C. Cutmer, 1st Lt. 812 W. Elk St. Harrysville

Gerald J. Doubley, 1st Lt. Warsaw, Ill.

Joseph E. Hanson, 1334 Baton Rouge, La. Mass.

Richard E. Coulaye, Palmer City, Mass.

R. Cy. Hill, Natchez, Miss. U.S.S. DICKMAN

F. Perry Williams, Lt. USBCR USS Dickman

E. L. Steward

www.ingramcontent.com/pod-product-compliance
Lightning Source LLC
Chambersburg PA
CBHW070510130626
46555CB00003B/1245